96

Who Runs Britain?

WHO RULES BRITAIN?

John Scott

Polity Press

Copyright © John Scott 1991

First published 1991 by Polity Press
in association with Blackwell Publishers
Reprinted 1992

Editorial office:
Polity Press, 65 Bridge Street,
Cambridge CB2 1UR, UK

Marketing and production:
Blackwell Publishers
108 Cowley Road, Oxford OX4 1JF, UK

238 Main Street, Suite 501
Cambridge, MA 02142, USA

ISBN 0 7456 0302 5
ISBN 0 7456 0563 X (pbk)

British Library Cataloguing in Publication Data
A CIP catalogue record for this book is available from
the British Library.

Library of Congress Cataloging in Publication Data
A CIP catalogue record for this book is available from
the Library of Congress.

Typeset in 10½ on 12 pt Times
by Photo·graphics, Honiton, Devon

Printed in Great Britain by T.J. Press, Padstow, Cornwall.

Contents

Illustrations

Boxes

Tables

Acknowledgements

The author and publisher are grateful to the following for permission to use and for their help in supplying photographs: the Worker's Movement Library, Stockholm (Plate 1.3); A. F. Kersting (Plate 3.1); Rodney Todd-White and Son and Her Majesty Queen Elizabeth II (Plate 3.2); Dr John B. Free, Heritage and Natural History Photography (Plate 4.1); Skyscan Balloon Photography Copyright (Plate 4.2); Mr S. Maybury (Plate 5.1); The Hulton Picture Company (Plate 6.2); Camera Press, London and Jon Blau (Plate 6.3). All other photographs are provided by the author.

Introduction

The view is widely held that in Britain there is a small minority which holds a ruling position in its economy, society, and political system. This minority has been described in numerous varying ways: 'the establishment', 'the powers that be', 'the ruling few', the 'elite', or, more prosaically, 'them'. Differing terminology reflects, in part, differing political perspectives on the nature and purpose of power. From both the right- and the left-hand sides of the political spectrum, critics and commentators have claimed to have identified a propertied elite whose members, for good or for ill, are able to determine the outcome of political decision-making and so to determine the overall direction of social development.

For commentators on the right, elite rule is not only natural and inevitable, it is beneficial to society. Rule by an elite is seen as a guarantee of liberty and justice against the threats to those principles posed by the habits and prejudices of the masses. What, from this point of view, is more desirable than that those with the greatest and most substantial stake in British society – those who actually own its land and productive resources – should be in a position to act in the public interest and to exercise a benign stewardship over public life? While property ownership occupies a central position in many of these views, a number of commentators from the right have seen property as a mere secondary feature of the elite. Instead, the elite is defined by its cultural role as a counterbalance to the threat of the mass society. Ruling positions are held by those who are the best-educated and the most cultivated, and it is on this basis that their authority can be justified.

Critics on the left, naturally enough, take a rather different view. Elite rule is deplored as a process through which the sectional privileges of one group are advanced at the expense of the interests of the majority, as a denial of the principles of democracy and citizenship. What, from this point of view, is more objectionable than that those who are least necessary for society to function – those who depend upon the exploitation of others – should be in a position to manipulate public affairs? Among the critics on the left are those who write from a Marxist point of view and see the ruling minority as a 'ruling class' rooted in the ownership and control of the means of production.

But such views are not the only perspectives on the distribution of political power in Britain. For many commentators – and not just for those in the centre of the political spectrum – there is no real elite. The language of privilege and division used by those on the left and the language of cultural superiority used by those on the right serve to create the impression of elite rule by reinforcing the image of Britain as a 'class-ridden' society. Underneath the rhetoric and the imagery, it is argued, is an open and egalitarian society which is distorted by its own self-perception in class terms. Political decisions are, of course, taken by a minority, but this is not seen as a self-perpetuating elite. In any complex society there will be a division of labour in which some people are involved in decision-making and administration while others are not. The so-called 'elite' comprises simply the current occupants of political office. The equality of opportunity which, it is held, characterizes British society ensures that there is easy and open access to these positions for all who wish to take them up. The electoral mechanisms of political democracy, furthermore, ensure that the majority can control the actions of the minority.

These contending viewpoints revolve around two major issues. On the one hand there is the question of whether the elite is a purely *nominal* category of office holders or a *real* and active social group. On the other hand there is the question of whether the members of the elite use their power for *sectional* or for *public* purposes. These questions have structured the debates which have set one social scientist against another and the research which has attempted to resolve the clash of theoretical positions. But these issues are not, however, matters of purely academic interest. It is, clearly, a matter of the first order to decide whether one's own society is ruled by a cohesive and self-perpetuating social grouping acting in pursuit of its own sectional interests, or by a temporary coalition of office holders who will act in the public interest and will, in due course, be replaced by another temporary coalition. On such issues revolve all manner of political choices and preferences.

Discussion of these problems has rarely reached any degree of sophistication. Much discussion has been cast in terms of the fate of the aristocracy.[1] The ruling minority of the nineteenth century is seen as an elite of large landowners with peerage titles – dukedoms, earldoms, viscountcies, and baronies – which gave them the right to sit in parliament. The break-up of the large estates and the declining significance of the House of Lords have, it is argued, led to a loss of power. The titled aristocracy is no longer an aristocracy of wealth, it is a diverse group of people who happen to have inherited titles but have little else in common with one another. Wherever power may reside today, it is held, it no longer rests with the landed aristocracy. Academic work which has elaborated this view includes the important study by William Guttsman,[2] who holds that the twentieth century has seen the decline of the 'upper class' and the rise of the 'middle class' as the principal source of political power. The recruitment of the political elite has substantially broadened since the nineteenth century.

Even if such views are accepted – and I shall question them at many points in this book – they have little to say about the actual mechanisms of political power in British society. Of much greater value, in this respect, have been the journalistic writings of Anthony Sampson,[3] which have been extremely influential in informed public opinion. Sampson accepts the view that the aristocracy can no longer be seen as a ruling minority and adds to this that there is no longer a real social elite at all. Drawing on interviews and on his own observations, Sampson concludes that the various hierarchies of British society have become gradually more open in their recruitment over the course of the twentieth century and that the diversity of hierarchies is such that there is no single centre of power.

But Sampson's work fails to place political power in its broader economic and social context, and so, in its turn, gives a rather partial view. Those who have attempted to rectify this situation have tended to be Marxist writers, among whom Ralph Miliband has been the most influential.[4] According to Miliband, Britain is ruled by a 'ruling class' made up of the owners and controllers of capital. While landownership may have declined in significance during the twentieth century, he argues, land remains an important form of capital and there is still a capitalist class in Britain today. Rooted in the ownership of stocks and shares as well as land, this class is a highly privileged social group with a superior standard of living and with the ability to monopolize access to all the hierarchies which make up the structure of power.

I shall agree with Miliband's view that there is in Britain today a ruling class, but I shall try to avoid a number of crucial theoretical problems which flaw his work. These problems centre around the concept of the ruling class itself. Although this is, in many respects, the central concept in Marxist theory, it has rarely been discussed with any rigour. Indeed, the term is used in such an elastic way that it is often difficult to see it as having any meaning or value at all. I believe that the term can be salvaged and seen for the useful concept that it is, only if its constituent elements are clarified. Unlike the terms 'elite' and 'minority' that I have used in this Introduction, the Marxist concept roots the exercise of political power in class relations. C. Wright Mills claimed that the phrase 'ruling class' combines the *economic* concept of class with the *political* concept of rule and that, for this reason, the hybrid term should be rejected.[5] My contention, on the other hand, is that this combination of elements makes it an extremely powerful idea.

I shall try to defend the relevance of the concept of a ruling class, but do not wish to defend the whole framework of Marxist theory. My theoretical framework draws on the work of both Weber and Marx. Specifically, I use Weber's analytical distinctions between class, status, and party as ways of clarifying the Marxian concepts of the capitalist class and the ruling class. 'Class', for Weber, involved the determination of life chances through the structure of property ownership and the operations of the labour and capital markets. 'Status', on the other hand, involved the determination of life chances through the distribution of prestige and the formation of definite styles of life and patterns of privilege.[6] The concept of 'party' was used by Weber as a general term to refer to political parties, trades unions, and other bodies which enter into political conflict. It was closely allied with the concept of 'elite', which was developed by Pareto and Mosca and was defined through the distribution of the means of organization, surveillance, and violence. Classes, status groups, and elites, therefore, can be seen as different elements in the overall distribution of power in society.[7]

Marx's concept of the ruling class was used by him and by his followers in a rather loose way, sometimes being seen simply as an unproblematic extension of the concept of the capitalist class, as a concept rooted in the economic dimension of class relations. But the idea of a ruling class raises crucial and distinct issues concerning the exercise of political power. The concepts of elite and party which were developed in the Weberian tradition are essential means for clarifying this idea. This was recognized by Miliband, who made extensive use of the concept of elite – indeed, he was much criticized for this by other Marxists, who felt that he should not have departed from the narrow framework of Marxist theory. But Miliband failed to distinguish the general notion of 'elite' from the more concrete concepts which are required for empirical research. In this book I shall use Miliband's concept of the 'state elite', but I add to this the important additional concepts of 'power elite' and 'power bloc'.

The book gives much attention to the question of social status. The hierarchy of status is seen as an important element in the legitimation of power structures, and the dynamics of status group relations are seen as integral elements in class reproduction and in the formation of power blocs. The status system can be visualized as a hierarchy of social circles, each circle comprising status equals with a similar style of life and, in many cases, privileges. In some circumstances the status hierarchy is headed by a single 'upper circle' of status superiors, while in other circumstances there may be a small set of intersecting upper circles. Thus, the concepts of 'capitalist class', 'upper circle', and 'state elite' are analogous terms for describing the advantaged groups in the exercise of power in the dimensions of, respectively, class, status, and politics. It is on this basis that I try to reconstruct the concept of the ruling class.

The title of this book, *Who Rules Britain?*, is a deliberate borrowing from Domhoff's important and influential *Who Rules America?*[8] Like Domhoff, my aim is to outline the structure of power which determines the overall direction in which British society has developed. I begin in chapter 1 with the economic dimension of 'class', and I set out the various meanings which have been given to the fundamental idea of the capitalist class. The chapter reviews Marxist, Fabian, and managerialist theories of class relations in capitalist society. I then turn, in Chapter 2, to the even more complex concept of the ruling class, reviewing orthodox and unorthodox Marxist theories and drawing on the traditions of elite theory to specify the key ideas. Chapter 3 uses these ideas to give a brief historical review of the making of the British ruling class, looking at some of the implications of the transition from the 'old society' of the eighteenth century to the 'modern' structure of Victorian Britain.[9]

The three remaining chapters of the book set out to answer the three key questions which arise when asking 'Who Rules Britain?' Chapter 4 asks 'Is there still a Capitalist Class?' This is of absolutely fundamental importance, as many writers have argued that Britain – like other 'industrial societies' – no longer has a capitalist class. In that chapter I review the evidence on this question and argue that it is still possible to recognize an economically dominant capitalist class at the top of the class structure. Chapter 5 asks 'Is there still an Upper Circle?', and is concerned with the shape of the status hierarchy. I argue that there has been an important shift in the structure of the status order. The capitalist class is no longer structured around a single upper circle, but comprises a series of overlapping under circles. Chapter 6, asking 'Is there still a Ruling Class?' grapples with the central concern of the book. The chapter restates the definition of the ruling class used in this book and shows how the participation of the capitalist class in the exercise of political power can be understood. It concludes that Britain does, indeed, have a ruling class.

I have endeavoured to make this book as accessible as possible to a wide audience. For this reason I have not cluttered the text with detailed footnotes and references. The works cited are, by and large, restricted to the most important and the most accessible sources.[10]

1 What is a Capitalist Class?

The idea of the capitalist class is rooted in both Marxist theory and in classical liberalism. In both traditions there is a recognition of a category of economic agents defined by their ownership and control of capital, the driving force of a capitalist economy. The capitalist class, from this point of view, has distinct and opposing interests to those of the other classes. In other theoretical traditions, however, the idea of a capitalist class is less easy to define. For many writers, social classes are hierarchically structured social groups which are defined in terms of their superior and inferior life chances. Max Weber and those influenced by him, for example, see social classes as social strata lying above and below one another in a stratification system. The geological metaphor of 'strata' gives meaning to the notion of a hierarchy with upper and lower levels. For Weber, propertied and commercial interests are among those generating 'positively privileged' social classes which stand in a superior position in the distribution of life chances.

This contrasting imagery is the basis of different views of class relations and class action. In the Marxist tradition, it is the structured antagonisms and contradictions of interests between class positions, and not any distributive inequalities of income, wealth, or life chances, which define class relations. These structural conditions are the basis of class conflict. According to Weber, however, there is no necessity for overt conflict to exist between classes. There may be various forms of cooperation and consensus, as well as divisions and conflicts.

In fact, the contrast between these two conceptions is not so stark as it appears, despite differences in terminology. Although 'capitalist class' and 'bourgeoisie' are, perhaps, the most widely used terms for the dominant class in Marxist theory, it is perfectly possible to reconcile these notions with the idea of hierarchically arranged social strata. My aim in this chapter is to expand on this claim and, in so doing, to build on the Marxist conceptualization and to fuse it with a hierarchical view of class. To this end, I shall review the work of some of the more important writers who have tried to use such ideas to document the changes which have occurred at the upper levels of the class system during the twentieth century.

The Orthodox Marxist View

Marx's own view of class has been hotly debated, owing to his failure to write a complete and comprehensive treatise on class. The concept of class is discussed most fully in *The Communist Manifesto*, written jointly with Engels, and in the unfinished third volume of *Capital*. But the discussion in *Capital* was not completed. Just as Marx began to set out a formal definition of class, his manuscript came to an abrupt end, and his readers are left with merely a few tantalising suggestions. But the concept of class, of course, permeates Marx's whole body of work, and its most general meaning is clear. Indeed, in many parts of his work, he spells out in some considerable detail the class relations which he believes to exist in particular societies.

Marx saw classes as defined by the ownership and non-ownership of the means of production, which gave control over the process of production and the finished product. This led him to an essentially dichotomous image of class relations: a person either does or does not have property. His reliance on a dichotomous view led him to stress the antagonistic relations of opposed classes. Indeed, he believed that class relations were becoming ever more simplified as the old hierarchies of status, tradition, and privilege gave way under the compelling force of capitalist modernization. He frequently wrote as if capitalist societies were evolving in the direction of a 'polarization' between capitalist class and working class, 'bourgeoisie' and 'proletariat', corresponding to the structural division between capital and labour. In *The Communist Manifesto*, published in 1848, Marx and Engels held that 'Society as a whole is more and more splitting into two great hostile camps, into two great classes directly facing each other: bourgeoisie and proletariat.'[1]

But in the famous, unfinished section of *Capital* his view is more complex. Marx identified what he termed the 'three great classes' of modern capitalism: 'The owners of mere labour-power, the owners of capital, and the landowners, whose respective sources of income are

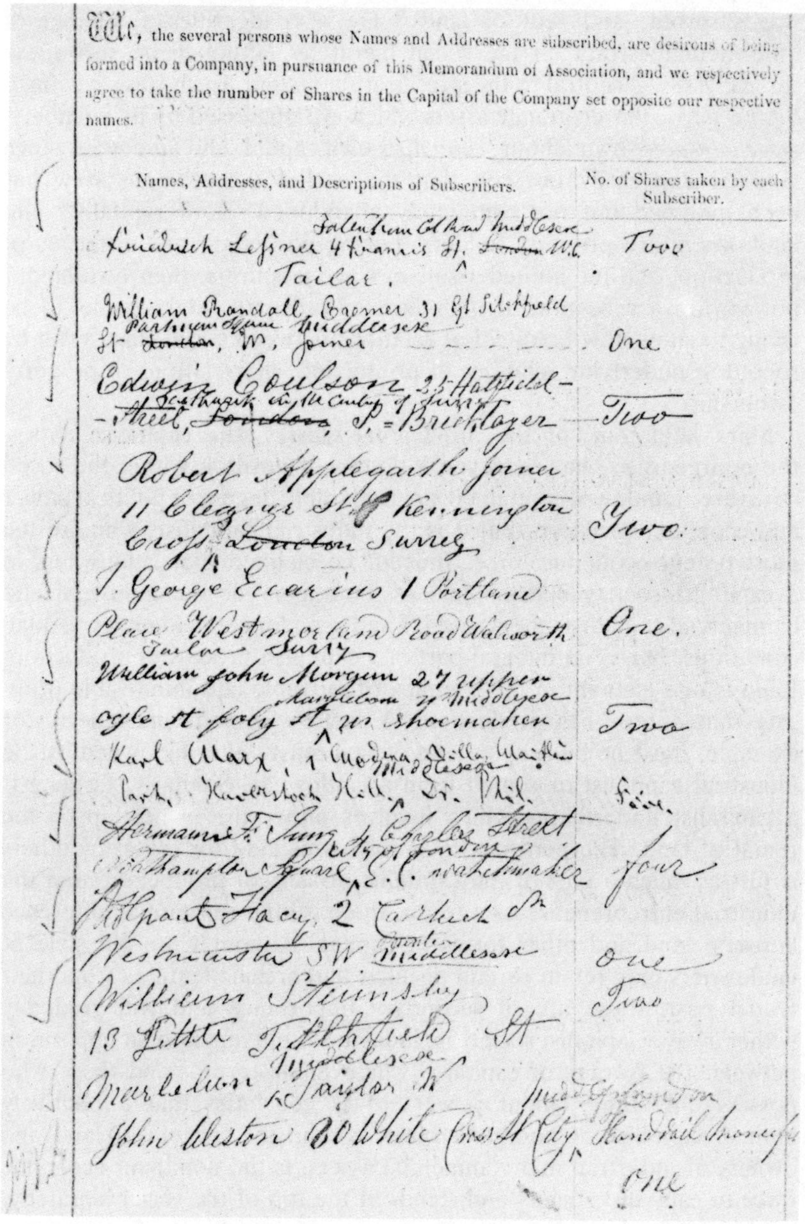

We, the several persons whose Names and Addresses are subscribed, are desirous of being formed into a Company, in pursuance of this Memorandum of Association, and we respectively agree to take the number of Shares in the Capital of the Company set opposite our respective names.

Names, Addresses, and Descriptions of Subscribers.	No. of Shares taken by each Subscriber.
[handwritten entries — see image]	

Plate 1.1 Karl Marx: Shareholder. The list of shareholders in *The Workman's Advocate*, 1865.

wages, profit, and rent of land'.[2] He also identifies a number of 'intermediate strata' in the social hierarchy, although he sees these three classes as central to the stratification system. Each class is defined by the particular economic assets which are possessed by its members: *wage labourers* own labour, *capitalists* own capital, and *landowners* own land. It can easily be seen that the earlier dichotomous view has been modified but not completely abandoned. Both capitalists and landowners are property holders, having possession of the means of production, and the limited assets of wage labourers, their own labour power, are a reflection of their lack of property. Marx seems to be trying to show how hierarchical relations between social classes can be rooted in underlying relations of production, the relations of property ownership.

Marx held that, of the three great classes, the capitalist class – the bourgeoisie – had achieved a dominant position within the social structure. Landowners retained a considerable degree of political power and economic privilege, but it is the industrial capitalists who are the most potent economic force. Indeed, he claimed that landowners in a capitalist society become just as 'bourgeois' as the industrial and commercial capitalists themselves. Land is no longer held under 'feudal' conditions, but as an integral part of a capitalist process of production. Land is one element in the complex of movable and immovable property that enters into production. A factory with its machinery, for example, must be built upon land, which must either be owned by the industrial capitalist or rented from a landowner. Similarly, farming is a capitalist undertaking which involves either the ownership or the rental of land. The person who simply owns land for rental by others is just as much a part of the capitalist process of production as is the industrial entrepreneur. As a result, there is little substantial difference between land and other forms of capital. Although the life style of landowners may retain certain peculiar and archaic features from their feudal past, these are of secondary importance and will gradually wither away. Capitalist society is, indeed, simplifying into an opposition between the owners of capital – whatever its form – and those who possess only their labour power. Marx concludes that a relatively unified capitalist or bourgeois class, comprising owners of land and owners of industrial and commercial assets, is the dominant economic force in capitalist society and stands at the top of the social hierarchy.

Marx recognized, however, in various parts of his work, that there were certain features of modern capitalism which were not adequately grasped by this view. In particular, he pointed to the growing importance of the joint stock company from the 1860s onwards. Its increasingly

Cartoon.

ELBOWING HIM OUT.

It is not only in the Shorthand world that the gentler sex are said to be gradually superseding male workers, for bookkeepers are now complaining that their sphere of labour is in a similar unsatisfactory state.

Plate 1.2 The Intermediate Classes: The feminization of clerical work, c.1900. (Author).

bureaucratic organization made the simple contrast between capitalist and worker a less realistic model for actual societies. The proliferation of managerial workers within the joint stock company involved an expanding 'intermediate' group within the class structure. Managers and clerks were propertyless, but they were differentiated sharply from proletarian wage labourers by virtue of their role in the service of capital and by the incomes which they were able to command. The rise of the joint stock company was also recognized by Marx to involve a change in the structure of property ownership, a development of fundamental significance for capitalist production. But Marx failed to pursue the implications of this for his conception of the capitalist class.

When production is organized through a joint stock company, the entrepreneur raises capital through the stock exchange – through the issue of shares – rather than relying simply on his or her personal resources. Capital is provided by a large mass of individual investors who buy shares in the company but have little or no say in how that capital is put to use. The expanding banking and credit system mobilizes this mass of savings and makes it available to capitalist enterprises. The capitalist can draw on a wider pool of money without giving up any control over the business. Bureaucratic managers in the service of the joint stock companies and the capitalists who run them play an increasingly important role in determining the pattern and pace of capitalist production; individual small shareholders play a correspondingly smaller part.

Later Marxists have attempted to work through the implications of these processes for the class structure of twentieth-century capitalism. Writers such as Renner and Hilferding were among the first to document the extremely rapid development of these processes in Germany, and they traced a parallel rise of substantial bank shareholdings. Small individual shareholdings, they argued, were supplemented by the large shareholdings which banks themselves took in large production and commercial undertakings. Banks used money deposited in bank accounts to buy large blocks of shares. Unlike the small shareholders, bank depositors did not even have a nominal title to the shares which the banks bought with their money. The banking mechanism was the culmination of the transformation of property begun in the joint stock company: it centralized massive amounts of money without transferring any rights of control to those who provided it. As a result, enterprises became more and more closely tied together in large and monopolistic bank-dominated groups. The competition of individual enterprises was replaced by the rivalries of competing financial 'empires'. Those people who ran the banks were able, without substantial personal shareholdings, to control massive conglomerations of capital. The major conclusion drawn by these writers was that the original capitalist entrepreneurs were being supplemented by 'finance capitalists' and by a bureaucratic 'service class'.[3]

Many non-Marxist writers have identified similar trends, but have seen them as resulting in the demise of the capitalist class. A capitalist class, they hold, is dependent on the *personal* ownership of business, and large-scale enterprise has broken beyond the bounds of this purely personal ownership. Enterprises can no longer be financed by individual entrepreneurs and must, instead, rely upon large numbers of small

Plate 1.3 The Capitalist Hierarchy: A radical view. (Reproduced by kind permission of the Worker's Movement Library, Stockholm.)

shareholders, all of whom play a merely passive role in business. As small shareholdings increase in number, so the personal shareholdings of the capitalists become less significant. Where the capitalist could formerly hold on to a majority of the shares in a company, the increasing scale of production makes this unviable. The shareholdings of the original capitalists become as small and insignificant as all other shareholdings. Shareholding ceases to be a basis of economic power. 'Ownership', they argue, is divorced from 'control', and the powers of control are exercised by the 'middle-class' managers who fill the corporate bureaucracies of the large enterprises. The rigid and conflict-ridden class structure of the nineteenth century disappears, to be replaced by an open and flexible hierarchy centred around the massive and expanding middle classes.[4]

The most influential Marxist critic of this position as it applies to Britain is Sam Aaronovitch, who has advocated the continuing relevance of the concept of a capitalist class. Aaronovitch argues that the capitalist class has not disappeared; it has survived and prospered over the course of the twentieth century. The development of the joint stock company and the growth of the banking and credit system have not destroyed the link between ownership and control, they have merely changed its character. Drawing on the insights of writers such as Hilferding, Aaronovitch argues that the growing involvement of banks, insurance companies, and other financial 'institutions' as lenders and as shareholders has created a tight fusion of banking and industrial capital, and has led to the creation of great conglomerates and combines which could not have been produced through personal family capital alone. Nevertheless, these huge concentrations of capital are still subject to private ownership and control. Not all their shareholders are small-scale, passive investors. On the contrary, the largest shareholders 'constitute collectively a decisive owning class'.[5] Some are 'absentee shareholders', while others are active directors, but they are all part of a propertied, capitalist class dominated by the 'finance capitalists' who direct many companies through an extensive system of interlocking directorships.

Aaronovitch instances the Cowdray, Rothschild, Samuel, and Oppenheimer families, together with the heads of large and impersonally owned groups and banks – Drayton, Bicester, Kindersley, Keswick, and so on.[6] The standing and power of the class of large property holders is buttressed by the tendency of banks, insurance companies, and other financial institutions to become major shareholders in companies themselves. The direct shareholdings of the finance capitalists are supplemented by the holdings of the institutions on

Table 1.1 *A Marxist view of British finance capital*

Banks	Boards connected to:		
	Top 50	Insurance	Other financial
Bank of England	GEC, AEI, Cadbury, Courtaulds	Northern, Royal Exchange, Equity & Law, Provident Mutual	Royal Bank of Scotland, Glyn Mills, Lazard, Hambros, London Electric Transport Finance
Midland Bank	J & P Coats, Ind Coope & Allsopp, Dunlop, ICI, GKN, Steel Co. of Wales, Powell Duffryn	London & Lancs.	ICFC, Philip Hill Investment
Lloyds Bank	Royal Dutch Shell, BICC, Vickers, Lucas, English Electric	London Assurance, National Provident, Midland Employers' Mutual, Phoenix, Sea, General, Yorkshire, Caledonian	Clive Discount, Alexanders' Discount, Robert Benson/Lonsdale
National Provincial Bank	Anglo-Iranian Oil, Ford, Imperial Tobacco, Tube Investments, Stewarts & Lloyds, Distillers, Burmah	Sun, Sun Life, Equitable Life, Prudential, Atlas, London Life, North British & Mercantile	Robert Fleming, Union Discount, Macneill Barry
Westminster Bank	United Steel, John Summers, P & O, Richard Thomas & Baldwins	Guardian, Employers' Liability, Commercial Union	Anthony Gibbs, Railway Finance, British Wagon
Martin's Bank	Cunard		Edw. de Stein
District Bank	Turner & Newall, Lancashire Cotton	Royal, Liverpool London & Globe	
Barclays Bank	Furness Withy	Aviation & General, Economic, Whitehall, World Auxiliary	

Source: summarized from S. Aaronovitch, *Monopoly*, p. 56. The data relate to 1951.

whose boards of directors they sit. (See table 1.1). The capitalist class of the mid-twentieth century, therefore, comprises a small oligarchy of finance capitalists – the 'giant sharks' in the corporate sea – and a great mass of their small and medium-sized propertied dependants.

The Fabian View

The orthodox Marxist claim that the capitalist class has survived and prospered in the face of the transformation of capitalist production is echoed in the work of the early Fabian writers at the turn of the century. George Bernard Shaw was strongly influenced by Marxist ideas, and he and Sidney Webb worked these ideas into a non-Marxist theory which became the basis of a central tradition in British socialist thought. They saw their central tasks as those of education and the provision of information in the struggle for socialism, and, through the Fabian Society they were centrally involved in the formation of the *New Statesman* and the founding of the London School of Economics.

Fabian social theory came to comprise the core of the 'social democratic' or 'ethical socialist' tradition in British social thought, represented most strongly in the inter-war years by Tawney. Through the works of its founders and those influenced by them, and especially through its association with the LSE, Fabian social theory became a major influence on the development of British sociology in the inter-war and post-war period.[7]

The Fabians saw class relations as permeating the whole gamut of advantages and disadvantages in society, forming a complex hierarchical structure of inequality. In this respect they came close to Weberian ideas. They followed the mainstream of Marxist writing, however, in seeing the foundation of the class structure in the economic relations of private property. The basic division in capitalist society, they argued, was between those who own and control the means of production and those who do not. This is the basis of the division between a *privileged* class of rich property owners and a *proletarian* class of routine workers. As Shaw characteristically expressed it, there was a class polarization between 'large appetites and no dinners at one extreme, and large dinners and no appetites at the other'.[8]

Since the position of the privileged class of plutocrats was rooted in the structure of private property, it followed that changes in the structure of property ownership would have important implications for class relations. From the late nineteenth century, joint stock businesses had tended more and more to amalgamate into large monopolistic combinations which operated on a national and international scale. These monopolies enabled firms to mobilize other people's savings in order to increase their own size and to minimize competition in the economy. As a result, the old-style capitalist entrepreneur was giving way to a new kind of capitalist.

The monopoly enterprises had created a separation between those who fulfilled the pure role of capitalist, and those who supplied the organizational and business ability required by the large-scale undertakings. There had emerged a role differentiation from the entrepreneurial capitalist employer into the dual roles of capitalist and manager. The purely capitalist role, moreover, had itself become differentiated into the dual roles of 'shareholder' and 'financier'.

This role differentiation, however, did not enhance the power of managers. Ownership of shares and control over finance remained highly concentrated as a basis for continuing capitalist power. The managers in large-scale organizations were part of a subordinate 'intellectual proletariat'. Shareholders and financiers, on the other hand, formed the core elements in a transformed capitalist class. Although the capitalists had, in a sense, become unnecessary to the process of production – which could be operated by the managers – the capitalists remained in ultimate control. The Fabian position gave a characteristic moral evaluation to this: while entrepreneurial capitalists were 'socially useful' and received the 'wages of superintendence', the new capitalist shareholders and financiers were a 'useless possessing class' of 'idle dividend receivers'. Though unnecessary for the process of production, their power remained entrenched. Unless and until the state intervened to remove capitalists, the useless class would retain their power.

The Fabians paid special attention to the position of financiers within this capitalist class. Bankers and other financiers who controlled access to the stock exchange and lending system, were able to determine which firms could obtain capital and under what conditions. For this reason, they were recruited to the boards of directors of all those companies which sought to expand and to build industrial monopolies. At the same time, the financial system itself was becoming increasingly monopolized. As a result, there emerged among corporate directors 'a tiny knot of bankers', a group of 'financiers and bankers who monopolise the art of collecting millions of spare money'.[9]

Figure 1.1 outlines the Fabian view of class structure. The propertied class dominates the rest of the class structure primarily through the relations between directors and managers. Within the group of company directors, however, the small core of financiers plays the key role in determining the flow of capital and, thereby, in determining the conditions under which other enterprises must operate. The directors and financiers are recruited from a larger pool of passive shareholders whose stance towards the business system is purely that of *rentiers* – they draw their income from their investments without having to undertake any actual work themselves. The stance of the rentier capitalists, therefore, is analogous to that of landowners to the use of their land, and the Fabians see a progression in the fusion of land and industry into an extensive 'plutocracy' which they characterize, following Veblen, as a 'leisure class'.[10] Britain exhibits 'the rule of the rich', though leisure ultimately prevails over activity: 'Those who try to make life one long holiday find that they need a holiday from that too.'[11]

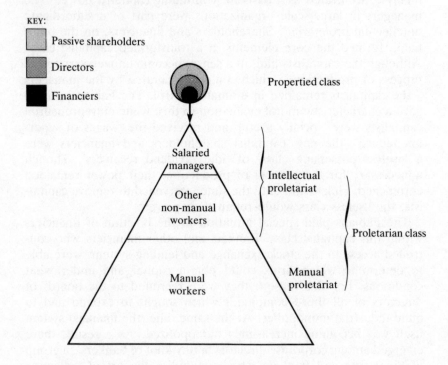

Figure 1.1   The Fabian view of class structure

Burnham and the Managerial Revolution

The main alternatives to Marxist and Fabian views, I have shown, see managers as the inheritors of powers formerly exercised by capitalists. Changes in the structure of business enterprise have led to the disappearance of the capitalist class and have brought about a 'managerial revolution'. The inspiration behind this idea was James Burnham, an American ex-Marxist who sought to argue that the Marxist analysis of control over the means of production was in serious need of modification.[12] According to his view, the developments highlighted by the orthodox Marxist and Fabian writers were simply the final, transient stage of capitalism. In this, of course, he was in accord with Marxist views. Burnham argued, however, that capitalism would be overthrown not by the proletariat but by the rising class of powerful managers. The managers would displace the capitalist class to become a new ruling class. While some earlier writers had proposed related ideas and had begun to pursue research into business ownership and control, Burnham's work set the research agenda for much modern writing on economic power.

Burnham's starting point was that private property is simply one possible basis for control over the means of production. 'Control' in the economic sphere consists of the power to determine who shall have access to the means of production and, consequently, the power to secure privileges and advantages from the distribution of the benefits of production. His claim was that this control was passing out of the hands of property owners. In the second half of the twentieth century, the technically qualified but propertyless managers have achieved such control. The basis of this managerial power is their technical qualifications, which enable them to undertake the essential tasks of direction, organization and coordination.

Technical changes in industry, argued Burnham, have eliminated the role of the capitalist entrepreneur. In a similar vein to the early Fabian writers, Burnham argues that the old style entrepreneur has been replaced, through role differentiation, by *shareholders* (who provide capital), *financial executives* (who undertake the task of planning for profitability), and *managers* (who are responsible for the technical coordination of production). In the latest stage of capitalist development emerged the *finance capitalists*, whose role was to centralize the funds of individual shareholders and to make them available to industry through the stock exchange and banking system.

Both shareholders and finance capitalists, argued Burnham, are marginal to the actual process of production. They are surplus to requirements. The financial executives are rather more closely linked to the day-to-day production of goods, but their concern is purely with the production of profit for property. All three groups, therefore, are inextricably linked with the framework of capitalist private property and are dependent on its continuation. The interests of the managers, on the other hand, are independent of property relations. The complexity of modern production methods requires people with the technical skills and competence which enable them to understand, and so to control, the process of production. There is, therefore, a division of interest between the managers and those committed to the system of property.

There is, at the same time, a partial separation between, on the one hand, control over access to and use of the means of production and, on the other hand, the ability to benefit from this production. While managers have become an indispensable controlling element in modern production, it is the shareholders, finance capitalists, and finance executives who gain the most advantages from the ways in which the system operates. But Burnham saw this as destined to change. The position of managers would continue to improve, even within the framework of capitalist private property, as capitalists become increasingly superfluous and managers become increasingly indispensable.

Burnham added to this argument the claim that the rise of managers was reinforced by the voluntary withdrawal of capitalists. Finance capitalists and wealthy shareholders, he argued, have increasingly preferred a life of 'leisure' and participation in 'Society' to the daily grind of making money. As a result, they have come to give less of their time to supervising the managers. The capitalist pursuit of leisure, therefore, enhances the power of managers. The managerial revolution will be complete when managers use the power of the state to consolidate their position and to remove the last vestiges of capitalism and the capitalist class. Writing in the 1940s, Burnham saw this managerial revolution as imminent.

Post-war Revisionism

The election of a majority Labour government in Britain in 1945 heralded an optimistic political period in which it was widely believed that the kind of society described by the Fabians and by orthodox Marxists was destined to disappear. Burnham's managerial revolution was about to be completed. The failure of the Labour party to be re-elected in 1951 triggered a series of investigations into the causes of electoral failure. A particularly influential strand of thought held that changes which British capitalism had undergone in the middle of the twentieth century had made the Fabian image of society increasingly unrealistic. Class relations had already changed, and the 'class' image of Labour had become an electoral liability.

Key texts in this 'revision' of social theory came from writers associated with the mainstream of Fabianism itself. Tawney's 1951 'Epilogue' to his *Equality* showed his attempt to rethink some of his own arguments about the overall shape of the stratification system and the opportunities available to the working class, and this became a major inspiration for David Glass's study of social mobility.[13] G. D. H. Cole had begun to move away from the mainstream of Fabianism in the 1930s, and the essays in his *Studies in Class Structure* were of great importance in re-directing attention away from the capitalist class and towards the analysis of 'elites'.[14]

Cole's argument was that the 'upper class' of the nineteenth century had been a hereditary landed gentry, based around a core of peers and baronets. The 'middle class' of the nineteenth century, on the other hand, was a new class rooted in trade and industry. At the core of this middle class were the capitalist entrepreneurs, but it was not a simple capitalist class. Based around the rich industrialists, the middle class stretched out to include managerial workers, subordinate employees, and tradesmen. This diverse group 'emerged distinctively as a middle class, conscious of their difference both from the gentry and from the main mass of the people below their economic level'.[15] The political developments of the nineteenth century, argued Cole, were an outcome of the relations between the upper, middle, and working classes. The middle classes achieved a form of accommodation with the landed upper class just at the point at which the middle class itself was expanding rapidly. The 'new' professionals and the clerical workers in the large-scale enterprises swelled the ranks of the middle class, and so the nineteenth century ended with a balance of power between a declining upper class and an expanding middle class.

By the middle of the twentieth century, argued Cole, the upper class was much shrunken and 'as a social class of really national significance, the upper class has nearly ceased to exist.'[16] It persisted as an archaic status group of landowners and members of the peerage, but it was no longer a powerful social class. Some of those whose wealth still came from landownership and farming had maintained their position by merging with the wealthier elements in the middle class. As a result, there was an 'upper middle class' of the really rich, based on wealth from industry or land. This new dominant class was economically separate from both the profit-making entrepreneurial middle class of small businessmen and the salaried middle class of technical, professional, and clerical workers. All of these middle classes, of course, were separated from the manual working class.

For Cole, then, the capitalist class had only ever formed part of a larger middle class. By the middle of the twentieth century, the various groups identified by the early Fabians had become part of a loose 'upper middle class', which contained all those who were involved in the exercise of economic power. Other writers, most particularly Anthony Crosland, went on to argue that the upper middle class had, in fact, become a managerial class in which property was of little significance.

Crosland's work was a major shaping influence on British sociology in the 1950s and 1960s.[17] He argued that the Marxist-inspired Fabian view had been largely accurate until the 1930s: there had, indeed, been a capitalist business class which dominated production and distribution. But this class, and its inner group of financiers, had, by the 1950s lost its power. The separation of 'ownership' from 'control' became a reality and destroyed the powers of the propertied. The previously subordinate salaried managers had been able to enhance their power in industry. Nationalization and the increased role of government in planning had, furthermore, transferred many of the 'levers of economic power' to the state, which had, in turn, become more responsive to the whole electorate. As a result, the state had pursued strategies of greater income equality through a greater willingness to impose heavy taxation on property.

Managers – the 'organization men' and technical experts – had become increasingly indispensable, for the reasons identified by Burnham, and they were able to supplant the weakened business class at the top levels of the major companies. In both the public and the private sector, salaried managers became the most important economic force. Managers were far less committed to profits than were the capitalist shareholders and financiers. They saw profits as the source of funds for growth, and so adopted a wider and more long-term perspective on business operations.

The managerial revolution in industry, combined with the decay of the old business class, were the harbingers of a new form of social structure in Britain. But Crosland's view of the managerial society differed from that of Burnham. Instead of forming a new dominant class, the managers were seen by Crosland as a beneficent social class well integrated into the wider social structure. The stratification system, argued Crosland, had become less polarized and more 'open'. The upper middle class identified by Cole was a managerial and professional class whose interests were not fundamentally opposed to those of the other classes. Managers and workers alike had common interests in the success of a growth-oriented and affluent economy which provided the basis for a more egalitarian society.[18]

The Capitalist Class Reconsidered

I have reviewed a number of views on the question 'What is a capitalist class?' All seem agreed that a capitalist class is defined by the advantages which derive from the ownership and control of property. The various theoretical positions differ, however, in their views on the pattern of ownership and control in modern capitalism and in the conclusions that they draw from these changes. Orthodox Marxism, for example, sees the changes as having produced a stronger basis for the survival of a capitalist class in the twentieth century. Burnham and Crosland, on the other hand, believed that the transformation of property had resulted in the decline of the capitalist class, though they differed in their views about what kind of class had replaced it.

What conclusions can be drawn from these discussions? Social classes must be seen as clusters of households which stand in a similar position with respect to the distribution of income and wealth and the overall distribution of life chances. Their members owe their advantages and disadvantages to their occupancy of specific *economic locations* among which mobility is both easy and frequent. Members of a particular class are divided from those of other classes, rooted in different economic locations and, therefore, experience distinct patterns of advantage and disadvantage. There is in Britain today a capitalist class whose members owe their advantaged life chances to the occupancy of capitalist economic locations. What distinguishes this class from the capitalist classes of the past are the specific locations that its members occupy in the modern capitalist economy.

Changes in the legal and financial structure of business enterprise have, indeed, had important implications for the contemporary class structure. But far from leading to the disappearance of the capitalist class, these changes have resulted in its transformation. It remains a centrally important feature of contemporary British society. It is a class whose members are dependent on the success of the system of capitalist private property which produces its income and wealth.

These conclusions must, of course, be substantiated, and I shall review the relevant evidence on these matters in Chapter 4. Before going into such issues, however, it is necessary to consider the larger question of the nature of a *ruling class*, and this will be the task of the following chapter.

2 What is a Ruling Class?

In the Marxist theory, the capitalist class is also seen as a ruling class. In the famous words of Marx and Engels in *The Communist Manifesto*, 'the bourgeoisie has at last . . . conquered for itself, in the modern representative state, exclusive political sway. The executive of the modern state is but a committee for managing the common affairs of the whole bourgeoisie.' And in *The German Ideology*, they add that 'the state is the form in which the individuals of a ruling class assert their common interests'.[1] The economically dominant class monopolizes the machinery of the state and uses it to pursue its own class interests; this constitutes it as a politically dominant class, a ruling class. All capitalist societies have capitalist ruling classes: the bourgeoisie rules throughout the capitalist world.

But Marx was clear that the situation in real societies would approximate to this pattern only in part. Just as the general tendency for class structures to become progressively more polarized had to be seen in relation to the more complex differentiation of class positions, so the general model of a ruling class had to be adapted to specific circumstances. The pattern of power in each particular society is unique and reflects its history and traditions. Later Marxist writers have sought to follow this same path of utilizing a general concept of the ruling class to grasp the concrete power arrangements of particular societies and periods. It is through considering Marx's own ideas and the views of those who have pursued their implications that a defensible concept of the ruling class can be developed.

Marx on the British Ruling Class

In his early work, it was the political situation in France to which Marx gave most attention, and this interest continued throughout his life. But in the 1850s and 1860s, at the same time as he was writing *Capital*, he turned his attention to Britain. In a series of occasional pieces he attempted to describe the class basis of political power in Britain. Marx, like other contemporary commentators, was well aware that the landed aristocracy continued to play a central role in political rule in British industrial capitalism. Palmerston's ministry of 1855, for example, was widely criticized in the press for being the most aristocratic administration in history, and Marx commented wryly that 'The outcry against the aristocracy has been answered ironically by Palmerston with a ministry of ten lords and four baronets, eight of the former sitting in the House of Lords.'[2] The aristocracy was not one merely of landowners, however. Its ranks included many wealthy financiers and merchants from the City of London; but it included no industrialists. Britain was a society in which the landed aristocracy and the 'financial aristocracy' prevailed over the claims of industry. Land and finance were united through myriad economic and personal bonds. In recruitment to the church, the army and the navy, as well as to the great offices of state, 'family connections and ready cash are the two factors that count'. Nevertheless, the growing political challenge of industrialists and a limited reform of the political system had led to a political compromise between land, finance and industry. In Britain there was 'a compromise between the class that rule officially and the class that rule non-officially'[3]: 'the general governing power is abandoned to some sections of the middle class, on condition that the whole of the real Government, the Executive in all its details, even to the executive department of the legislative power – or that is, the actual lawmaking in the two Houses of Parliament – is secured to the landed aristocracy.'[4]

The compromise was, however, unstable; the constitution was in crisis. The old pattern of parliamentary management, through which a stable system of political rule had been established, had broken down in the face of industry and reform, and MPs were divided into 'numberless fractions, attempting all the arithmetical combinations and variations of which a given number of units is capable'.[5] No stable re-alignment of politics had been established, and coalition after coalition fell.

In the middle of the 1850s, Marx saw this political crisis as representing the last gasps of the old society of the eighteenth century. The political crisis would generate working-class political discontent, he believed, and this would, in turn, force the industrial bourgeoisie into a more active political stance. The days of the aristocracy were numbered. But both Marx and Engels became increasingly pessimistic about the role of the workers in forcing this restructuring. In 1858 Engels wrote that 'the English proletariat is actually becoming more bourgeois, so that this most bourgeois of all nations is apparently aiming ultimately at the possession of a bourgeois aristocracy and a bourgeois proletariat *as well as* a bourgeoisie', and in 1863 Marx wrote of the 'bourgeois infection' which characterized the workers.[6] Marx and Engels also recognized that the enfranchisement of certain sections of the working class had reinforced the class alignment which ruled the state, as the workers deferred to the established social orders rather than challenging them: 'Everywhere the proletariat is the tag, rag and bobtail of the official parties.'[7] Thus, the accession of the industrial bourgeoisie did not result in the overthrow of the landed aristocracy from its established position in British society.

In Marx's work, therefore, we find two connected frameworks of analysis: a general model of the ruling class, and a concrete description of the class distribution of power in Britain. If the assumption of an inexorable simplification of class relations is rejected, the relationship between these two frameworks is unclear. When a complex alignment of classes share in the exercise of power, it is difficult to apply the general concept of a single ruling class. This problem has beset all subsequent Marxist attempts to analyse the ruling class.

The Orthodox Marxist View

Recent Marxist writers have continued the struggle to understand the involvement of finance capitalists and entrepreneurial capitalists alongside landowners in the exercise of political power. A major concern has been to incorporate an understanding of the changes in class structure which were discussed in the previous chapter. Haxey's analysis of the 1930s illustrates this well.[8] He showed that the Conservative party, the government, the civil service, the law and the military, were all recruited from an extremely narrow class background. Conservative MPs, for example, were drawn from the

wealthiest sections of society, many being millionaires or near-
millionaires. In particular, he argued, they were recruited from
business families, were themselves large shareholders, or were
actively involved as directors of industry. Above all, those who were
associated with the 'Big Five' clearing banks, the merchant banks
of the City, and the insurance companies 'go in and out of the
leading positions in the Conservative party and the government'.[9]

The wealthy social background of the ruling class is reinforced
by their shared experience of education in the major public schools,
and especially at Eton and Harrow. Haxey claims that 'these schools
are the most important training-ground for prospective Conservative
politicians. They are a part of a series of institutions which develop
the mental outlook of Tory legislators'.[10] It was their shared background and their connections which reinforced their unity of belief
and action.

Haxey also pointed to the continuing role of the peerage in the
state. Directly through the House of Lords, and indirectly through
the presence of members of its families in the House of Commons,
the peerage remained extremely important. They do not, however,
constitute a distinct social class. The peerage itself consists of the
leading elements in the *fusion* of landed, financial and industrial
interests. Many peers are recently ennobled industrialists and bankers, and others descend from nineteenth-century financiers. Through
its kinship links the peerage is intimately connected with the wider
circles of party and government, and at its core there is an extensive
'cousinhood' of governing families.

Aaronovitch, writing in the 1960s, came to very similar conclusions. He points to the growth of finance capital and claims that
'the finance capitalists may truthfully be described as the ruling class
if in fact the crucial political and economic decisions are taken by
their representatives and in their interests'.[11] The ruling class is
simply that section of the capitalist class which runs the state or in
whose interests others may operate it. This general argument, he
believes, can be applied to Britain, and he claims that 'We therefore
have Cabinets and Cabinet Committees led by and composed of
businessmen . . . continuously drawing in their colleagues from
finance and industry for consultation and decision-making. [These
Committees] represent the main forums (clubs and dinner parties
aside) where finance capital can decide State policy, reconcile conflicting interests or win out over rivals.'[12]

Aaronovitch argues that this web of power stretches out from the
centre of government to public authorities such as the BBC, the

Independent Television Authority, and the nationalized industries, and to the civil service. All the organs of the state are held and controlled by finance capitalists and their families. Even those in less important areas, such as the Administrative Class of the civil service, 'come mostly from the fringes of those families – the poor relations one might say'.[13]

The basis of Aaronovitch's claim is that class relations have altered in the direction anticipated by Marx. Land, industry and finance have come closer together into a single class dominated by the finance capitalists. His description of Britain's concrete patterns of rule, however, imply that there is an exclusive dominance of the finance capitalists. Power is not exercised by all sections of the capitalist class, but by its *dominant segment*.

The orthodox Marxist position, therefore, continues to employ the classical idea of the ruling class, but it applies this to a situation where land, industry and banking have fused under the dominance of finance capitalists. The 'ruling class' turns out to be only a segment of the capitalist class as a whole. The contradiction between the general model and the concrete pattern of power observable in British society is resolved by ignoring the conceptual ambiguity that this involves: how can a whole class 'rule' if positions of power are monopolized by a minority within that class?

An Unorthodox Marxist View

Ralph Miliband has put forward an influential and sophisticated reformulation of the classical Marxist position, using some of the findings and arguments of non-Marxist sociologists to overcome the more crude and mechanistic elements of the orthodox Marxist model. In doing so, he makes the further important point that those capitalists who participate in power generally do so alongside members of other classes. It is only very rarely that there is 'direct and sovereign rule by businessmen' as such'.[14] Under normal circumstances the capitalist class and the 'state elite' are separate entities: the capitalist class may be well-represented in the elite, but it is not the only class to be represented there. Those actively involved in business frequently express their disinterest or distaste for politics, and they may resent the intervention of politicians and civil servants in their affairs. For this reason, there is often a separation between 'politics' and 'business'. Miliband argues, however, that this is not to be taken as evidence against the idea of a ruling class:

The notion that businessmen are not directly involved in government and administration (and also in parliamentary assemblies) is obviously false. They are thus involved, ever more closely as the state becomes more closely concerned with economic life; wherever the state 'intervenes', there also, in an exceptionally strong position as compared with other economic groups, will businessmen be found to influence and even determine the nature of that intervention.[15]

Miliband forwards his argument by retreating from the classical Marxist view that the capitalist class rules by direct and exclusive participation in the state, but, at the same time, he all but abandons the very idea of a capitalist class. Following a similar line to that of Cole, his argument is that capitalist business leaders come from the 'upper and middle classes', from which the state elite is also drawn.

Modern capitalist societies, he argues, are dominated by an economy of giant corporations. There is still a small group of wealthy people which is able to control the assets of these corporations. These owners and controllers of the corporate economy – the capitalists – co-exist with small business owners and professional workers to constitute 'the propertied and professional classes' or the 'upper and middle classes'.[16] There is, therefore, a 'plurality of economic elites', each with distinct interests, but which nevertheless constitute a 'dominant economic class, possessed of a high degree of cohesion and solidarity, with common interests and common purposes which far transcend their specific differences and disagreements'.[17]

A similar argument has been put forward by Westergaard and Resler. They claim that a dominant class of directors, managers, professionals, and officials is separated from the mass of ordinary manual and non-manual wage earners by an 'intermediate cluster' of supervisors, technicians, and lower professionals. The latter constitute a 'social and political buffer group between the dominant class and the working class'.[18]

In this unorthodox Marxist position, recruits to the higher levels of the state apparatus are overwhelmingly drawn from this 'dominant class', though not exclusively from its purely capitalist component. Those who are responsible for recruitment and promotion within the state are themselves members of the upper and middle classes, and so they inevitably tend to draw new recruits disproportionately from those same classes. In consequence, 'the men [*sic*] who have manned *all* command positions in the state system have largely, and in many cases overwhelmingly, been drawn from the world of business and property, or from the professional middle classes'.[19]

The dominant class, as a result, controls the means of production, coercion, and persuasion. They are a ruling class 'in charge of the main institutions through which power, responsibility, and influence are mainly exercised'.[20] But Miliband uses the phrases 'ruling class' and 'dominant class' very loosely. The capitalist class becomes submerged in a wider 'dominant class', or 'upper and middle class', and the concept of 'ruling class' itself merges imperceptibly into such concepts as 'power elite' and 'establishment'. Miliband treats the terms 'ruling class' and 'dominant class' as virtually interchangeable.

In his most recent book on this topic, *Capitalist Democracy in Britain*, Miliband fails to clarify this conceptual confusion and ambiguity. The distinction between 'class' in the Marxist sense and 'class' in the sense of position in a social hierarchy is ignored, and the usage of 'dominant class' to describe owners, controllers, managers, professionals, civil servants, judges, and so on, glosses over virtually all the key distinctions which need to be made. In particular, the distinction between 'class' and 'state elite' which figured centrally in *The State in Capitalist Society*, disappears altogether. Although much of what he reports about the nature of the power distribution in British society is informative, the way in which he conceptualizes this material is inadequate and ultimately fails to convince.

The Power Bloc and the State

The classical idea of the 'ruling class' involved two distinct claims. First, that the capitalist class has a disproportionate representation in the exercise of political power, and, second, that the state operates in the class interests of capitalists to sustain and support their economic dominance. Both of these claims are essential to the classical idea. Many of the conceptual ambiguities which are to be found in the works of later writers result from a failure to appreciate the distinctiveness of these two claims. This results, in part, from an accident of translation. Marx's term *Klassenherrschaft* has most frequently been translated simply as 'class rule' or 'ruling class', though this phrase is rather better translated as 'class dominance'.[21] Marx introduced the term to describe the general framework of power through which an economically dominant class is able to rely on the continued guarantee of its economic position by the state. But it is clear from Marx's discussion of the concrete arrangements of power in British society that he also wished to direct attention to the actual extent of the involvement of members of the dominant class in the exercise of state power. This distinction can best be understood by distinguishing the general question of *political dominance* from the narrower issue of *political rule*. While political dominance refers to the overall framework of state power, political rule involves an active and deliberate influence over state decision-making.

This distinction can help to clarify a number of disputes in this area. Poulantzas' criticism of Miliband's position, for example, can be seen as a claim that Miliband's analyses of the processes of political rule through which different groups become involved in decision-making are irrelevant to the question of class domination. In Poulantzas' view, the political dominance of the capitalist class does not depend on involvement in political rule, it is a necessary consequence of the structure of the capitalist state.[22] Miliband's response to this point was that it is unlikely that class domination would persist for any period without some degree of involvement of the capitalist class in political rule. Without, at this stage, prejudging the outcome of this dispute, it is important to recognize that political domination may be a *necessary* condition for the existence of a 'ruling class', but it is not a *sufficient* condition. In order to be regarded as a true ruling class, a capitalist class must also be disproportionately represented in the machinery of political rule.

I shall return to these issues in a later chapter. For the moment, it is simply necessary to clarify what is meant by involvement in political rule and to suggest how this can best be explored. The apparently straightforward claim that a particular class is disproportionately represented in the exercise of political power is in need of both clarification and elaboration.

This clarification can be achieved through some conceptual innovation. In particular, I shall define the concept of a *power bloc* and the related ideas of a *state elite* and a *power elite*. Although some societies may have a relatively egalitarian power structure, it is more typically the case that a particular alignment of social groups prevails in the leading positions of the state. This alignment of social groups is what I refer to as a power bloc. It is necessary to examine the composition of the power bloc which exists in any society and to uncover the balance of forces within it. The concept of a ruling class requires, as a minimum, that the power bloc be dominated by a capitalist class.

The concept of a power bloc comes from Gramsci, though it was popularized by Poulantzas.[23] It describes an alignment of social groups, generally under the dominance of one of them, which is able to monopolize the levers of political power in a society over a sustained period. A similar idea has been formulated by Westergaard and Resler, who refer to 'the central cluster of ruling interests' in a society.[24] The power bloc is an alignment of divergent and partially conflicting groups which are united through a common focus on the exercise of state power. The social groups which participate in a power bloc may be classes, class fractions, status groups, or ethnic groups, but their diversity is subordinated to their common alignment for the purpose of power. Although described as an alignment of groups, the limiting case of a power bloc is that in which a single class, or other group, has a monopoly of political power.

This concept of the power bloc is rooted in many of the ideas of the sociological tradition of 'elite' analysis, and its meaning can best be elaborated by considering these origins. The earliest statements of the sociological concept of an elite are to be found in the writings of Pareto and Mosca, who laid the foundations of what they hoped would be a complete alternative framework of political analysis to the Marxian model of the 'ruling class'. For these writers, the study of elites was an integral part of an anti-Marxist political and theoretical position. This is, indeed, one of the main reasons for hostility towards the concept by Poulantzas and many other Marxists. The concept of an elite, however, can be given a valid meaning and use within sociology, despite its ideological origins.

While it was Pareto who popularized the term 'elite', it was Mosca who provided the more sophisticated understanding of the role of organized minorities in the exercise of political power. Mosca rejected Marx's argument that the ruling class was rooted in economic relations, and proposed that the ruling class be seen as consisting of all the separate ruling minorities in a society, whatever their institutional basis. It was this concept which subsequent writers, in order to avoid confusion with Marx's ideas, have termed the 'elite'.

An elite can be seen, in its simplest sense, as comprising those who stand at the top of a particular hierarchy or who are in some sense 'the best' in their field. But Pareto introduced an important distinction between those elites which are 'governing elites' and those which are 'non-governing elites'. A governing elite, he argued, is one whose actions are fateful for the character and development of a whole society, while a non-governing elite is important merely in a particular specialized area. Politicians, for example, may form a governing elite, but top athletes would comprise a non-governing elite.[25] And in a similar vein, Mosca identified a 'political class' within the wider elite.

It is the notion of a governing elite which figured most centrally in Pareto's work, his particular concern being to analyse the specific skills and attributes which are required by members of governing elites. Social change, he argued, depends upon the changing balance of political skills in the governing elite and, ultimately, on the replacement of one governing elite by another. Pareto termed this shift in the composition of the governing elite the 'circulation of elites', and his concept of 'circulation' has set the research agenda for much recent research. Indeed, I shall argue that it is central to the analysis of the relationship between power blocs and state elites.

Perhaps the most useful attempt to reformulate the ideas of Mosca and Pareto and to strip them from their anti-Marxist framework, has been that of Giddens.[26] Giddens narrows down the general idea of an 'elite' to positions of formal authority. He argues that 'elite' is simply a descriptive designation for 'those individuals who occupy formally defined positions of authority at the head of a social organisation or institution'.[27] All hierarchically organized groups will, by definition, have an elite. By defining the concept in terms of formal *authority*, Giddens leaves open for investigation the question of the actual *power* of elites relative to non-elite members and to other elites. These matters, argues Giddens, are to be analysed empirically.

On this initial definition, therefore, not only the British Cabinet and the Central Committee of the Communist party of the Soviet Union, but also the executive committee of the British Sociological Association and the management committee of a local golf club are 'elites'. But Giddens builds on Pareto's distinction between governing and non-governing elites to argue that it is important to recognize differences in the 'institutional salience' of organizations. The state, for example, has a greater impact on the life chances of British citizens than does the BSA on its members. If our concern is with the distribution of power in society at large, argues Giddens, we should concentrate our attention on the elites in salient institutions and organizations. From this standpoint, there are two important social boundaries to define: the *horizontal* boundary between the elite and the non-elite within each organization; and the *lateral* boundary between organizations of high and low salience.

The 'elite' in society as a whole, according to Giddens, consists

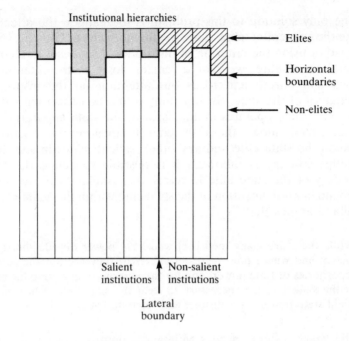

Figure 2.1 Elite boundaries

of all those who occupy leading positions in salient institutions –
the shaded area in figure 2.1. A crucial issue, however, concerns
where the horizontal and lateral boundaries are to be drawn in a
particular society. Giddens recognizes that they are, to some extent,
arbitrary, and he says simply that the lateral boundary should be
drawn in such a way as to 'spread the net as widely as possible'.[28]
In his own work, he fails to pursue these issues and merely takes
over many of the conventional definitions used in earlier elite
studies. The lateral boundary, for example, is drawn to include the
monarchy, the House of Commons, directors of the top 100 industrial enterprises, the judiciary, bishops, university vice-chancellors,
and so on. No justification is given for the inclusion or non-inclusion
of particular categories. Why, for example, include vice-chancellors,
but not newspaper editors? Giddens similarly makes a series of *ad
hoc* decisions about where to draw the horizontal boundary. The
civil service elite is said to comprise under-secretaries and above,
but not assistant-secretaries; the military elite comprises generals
and above, but not lieutenant generals; and the business elite
includes the directors of the top 100 industrials, but not the directors
of the next 100 largest companies; and so on.

The only solution to this problem is to abandon the attempt to make the concept of 'elite' quite so all-embracing as Giddens wishes. Instead of using the criterion of 'institutional salience' to identify a general social elite, we should remain closer to the intentions of Mosca and Pareto and focus our attention on the institutional hierarchies of the state. Such a study would be concerned with the *state elite* which operates in and through the state apparatus. Such a focus then allows the researcher to explore the relationship between the state elite and any other 'salient' elites in society.

If this strategy is followed, it is possible to define the lateral boundary of the state elite in terms very similar to those used by Miliband in his delineation of the state elite within the 'state system'. Miliband argues that

> While there are many men [*sic*] who have power outside the state system and whose power greatly affects it, they are not the actual repositories of state power; and for the purpose of analysing the role of the state . . . it is necessary to treat the state elite, which does wield state power, as a distinct and separate entity.[29]

The 'state system', argues Miliband, comprises five major areas of activity.[30] These are the *government, representative assemblies*, the *administration*, the *military and para-military* and the *judiciary*. The government is formally invested with state power and with the authority to act in the name of the state. In its widest sense, the government includes not only the central government but also semi-independent regional and local executive bodies. Similarly, representative assemblies include those at both the national and the local level.[31]

The state administration – essentially the civil service – is concerned with the actual management of the various activities in which the state is involved, and it is institutionally distinct from the other arms of the state.[32] The military and the para-military, argues Miliband, are concerned with the 'management of violence', and this branch of the state includes the army, naval and air forces, together with the security and police forces. They comprise the coercive arm of the state. Finally, the judiciary are constitutionally separate from the executive, but are direct servants of the state by virtue of their role in the court system.

The 'leading positions' in these various areas comprise the 'state elite'. The lateral boundary of the state elite, therefore, is easily defined if the boundaries of the state apparatus itself are used to identify the limits of formal state authority. The question of the horizontal boundary, however, is more difficult to resolve. A number of the institutional hierarchies of the state involve a continuous gradation of authority, and it is by no means obvious where the line is to be drawn between those inside and those outside the state elite. Positions within the state elite are those at the 'highest' levels of state authority – those concerned mainly with long-term strategy and planning rather than with day-to-day operations. The salience of the various positions within the state for these tasks may well vary over time and as the structure and activities of the state itself are transformed, so no horizontal boundary can be expected to serve as a universal feature of social structure. The horizontal boundary must be drawn by the researcher on the basis of an informed judgement of the nature of the positions and the tasks attached to them.

The state elite is defined as a category of offices, as formal positions of authority within the state. Those who occupy these positions at a particular time comprise a political elite. The state elite is a category of *positions*, while the political elite is a category of *people*.[33] All societies with a state elite, therefore, will have a political elite. But political elites can take different forms, and have varying degrees of openness and diversity of background. Where the political elite is strongly rooted in a power bloc, the political elite takes the form of a *power elite*. While all state societies will have a state elite, not all will have a power elite. The occupants of positions within the state elite comprise a power elite if they are recruited from a particular power bloc.[34] A power bloc, I have argued, is an alignment of social groups which is able to monopolize positions of authority within the state elite over a sustained period. It comprises a shifting balance of social groups whose unity is maintained by a compromise of interests and by the cultural unity which derives from a similarity of background and experience.

The patterns of dominance and subordination within the power bloc may also be maintained or transformed through the deliberate pursuit of strategies of alignment and closure. A dominant group may pursue a conscious and deliberate strategy of dominance within the power bloc. A landowning class which formerly exercised undisputed rule, for example, may seek to maintain its political power by seeking a broad alliance with 'new', rising classes, and it may seek to incorporate these other classes into a subordinate role. Concessions may be granted to the potential partners through *ad hoc* or implicit agreements, or perhaps by formal agreements, in an attempt to obtain their support. Such strategies of incorporation do not, of course, always work, and a dominant group may sow the seeds of its own destruction by aligning itself with a group which eventually undermines its dominance.

These patterns of dominance will be reflected in the degree of participation in political rule that the various groups are able to achieve. A dominant group will tend to be represented in the state elite to a much greater extent than its partners within the power bloc. For example, an aligned capitalist class, entrepreneurial middle class and service class may all be disproportionately represented in the state elite, but capitalist representation may be far more disproportionate to their numbers in society than that of the other two classes. Generally, disproportionate representation will involve a *relative* over-representation of one group, but in certain circumstances, this unequal representation may be such that the *absolute* number of people from one class exceeds the total number from all the other aligned groups. It is also important to recognize that the state elite is itself hierarchically structured, and that a dominant group may be disproportionately represented at the higher levels of the state elite. Members of the capitalist class may, for example, be represented more strongly in government than in parliament as a whole, and more strongly in Cabinet than in the government as a whole.[35]

In this chapter I have tried to show that the concepts of state elite, power elite, and power bloc enable us to examine the conditions under which a capitalist class may also be regarded as forming a ruling class. It is now possible to clarify the meaning of the concept of the ruling class itself. A capitalist class may be regarded as forming a ruling class when its economic dominance is sustained by the operations of the state and when, alone or through a wider power bloc, it is disproportionately represented in the power elite which rules the state apparatus.

These ideas will be elaborated more fully in Chapter 6, where I will argue that modern Britain has a power bloc which is dominated by its capitalist class. This power bloc is centred around a power elite which has been described as an 'establishment' and which has its political voice in the Conservative party. I shall also show that there is a community of interests within this power bloc and that the state's operations reflect this balance of interests. Within this balance, the interests of the capitalist class are paramount. To this extent, therefore, Britain does, indeed, have a ruling class.

3 The Making of the Ruling Class

The claim that Britain did, in the past, have a ruling class is far less contentious than the claim that it still has one today. The landed aristocracy of the eighteenth and nineteenth centuries was a capitalist class, albeit one rooted in agrarian rather than industrial capitalism. There is a widespread recognition that it formed a powerful and cohesive class which dominated the machinery of politics and whose ideas and values permeated the whole of British society. This view must, of course, be qualified by a recognition of the increasing economic and political power of industrial and commercial interests during the second half of the nineteenth century, a trend which is seen by some commentators as evidencing the overthrow of the ruling aristocracy. But the claim that the exercise of power in British society continued to disadvantage those outside the ranks of the propertied can hardly be questioned.

My aim in this chapter is to outline the relationship between land, commerce, and industry in Britain during the 200 years prior to the First World War, using the concepts developed in chapters 1 and 2. I shall show that Britain did, indeed, have a ruling class throughout this period. Having established this fact, it will be possible to consider twentieth-century Britain in the succeeding chapters.

Britain is a European society and its development has followed a similar course to the developmental trajectories found in other parts of western Europe. The formation of its capitalist class and the nature of their participation in political power are paralleled by patterns of class formation elsewhere. But Britain is, like any society, 'unique' in its historical inheritance. The British experience cannot simply be assimilated into some general developmental process. It is essential to highlight these unique features of class formation in Britain and to place them in their wider European context.

The *Ancien Régime* in Europe

The old societies of Europe – the *anciens régimes* – combined both 'pre-modern' and 'modern' features. They were a form of state and society in which certain 'modern' political and economic elements had been grafted on to a social structure which remained wedded to many of the practices of the medieval societies which had evolved from the period of classic feudalism.[1] By 'modern', in this context, is understood the capitalistic commercial practices of a market economy and the bureaucratic forms of political administration of a centralized nation state. These forms of economy and polity, which were to crystallize in their clearest forms only during the twentieth century, made their gradual appearance throughout western Europe in the period leading up to the eighteenth century.

The *anciens régimes* embodied this combination of archaism and modernity until the forces of modernity finally broke the archaic structure and, during the course of the nineteenth century, took the upper hand. Hobsbawm had characterized the sixty years from 1789 to 1848 as the period of the 'dual revolution': the French political revolution and the English industrial revolution. These two revolutions and their reverberations across Europe were the key elements in the transition from the old society to a fully modern society. The period of the dual revolution saw the beginnings of a transformation of the world, as the Franco-British transformation of Europe got underway. The modern forces of capitalist industry and bourgeois liberalism spread through Europe and laid the foundations for the creation of a world economic system dominated by the European imperial powers. By the end of the nineteenth century, much of Europe was fully modernized. Central to this growth of modernity was the expansion of the modern naval and military forces which enhanced the international power of the imperial states. It is hardly surprising that the 'long nineteenth century', from 1780 to 1914, which saw the transition to a fully modern society, should end in the first 'world' war.

The old societies of Europe were based around land and agriculture, though they showed varying degrees of mercantile and of urban development, and they differed in the extent to which agriculture had itself been commercialized. These societies were characterized by a co-existence of the rural economy and society of the countryside with the 'bourgeois' economy and society of the towns. Property and work relations in both agriculture and commerce were structured by kinship and similar particularistic and personal ties.

Although involving marked social inequalities and conflicts, the vertical bonds of 'patronage' were the cement which held the society together. For most people, and for most of the time, opportunities were acquired and help obtained through the mobilization of 'patrons' and personal contacts. The impersonal processes of the market and bureaucracy were complemented by the personal social networks of kin, friends, and neighbours, and by wider networks of tenants, servants, landlords, and political associates.

The old societies were also highly localized for most of their members. While the landed class and some 'bourgeois' groups had interests and activities at the national level, the local community was the focus of day-to-day interaction for the mass of the population. The national society as a whole and the activities of its leading members might be real and important to the upper classes, but the mass of the population had little conception of a society beyond the bounds of their own locality. The classical sociological idea of the *gemeinschaftlich* 'community' may overstate the homogeneity, cohesion, and consensus of localities in the old society, but it correctly grasps the central contrast with the forms of society which were to emerge in the nineteenth century.

The English old society – 'Britain' as a unit did not then exist – was undoubtedly the most commercialized and capitalistic in Europe. Its landed class was a capitalist class, with strong links to the merchant classes of the towns and cities. But the merchants, for their part, were not the purely urban 'bourgeoisie' that was to be such an important feature of many other European societies. English merchants were closely affiliated with the capitalist landowners, and there was a high degree of cultural uniformity in their outlooks. Where many European societies were structured by the contrast between a 'backward' and rural landed class and a 'progressive' and urban bourgeoisie, the English landed and commercial classes were united by a patrician, yet capitalist outlook on their activities.

The rural societies of Europe were all characterized by the differentiation between landlords, labourers, and farmers, but it was the form taken by the farming class that distinguished them most sharply. In England, northern Italy, and the Netherlands the farmers were capitalist producers – either tenant farmers or owner-occupiers, but all producing on capitalist lines for the market. In France and Germany, on the other hand, farming was predominantly the small-scale, subsistence concern of the peasantry. As a result, the English landlords tended to regard their estates as units of capitalist enterprise. They lived as 'rentiers' on the rents from their tenanted

farms and so were completely dependent on the successful application of capitalist principles in agriculture.[2]

Because of the political upheavals of the seventeenth century,
eighteenth-century England was no longer an 'absolutist' society
like France, but was effectively ruled by a patrician oligarchy of
landowners and financiers. Land and finance in England were the
basis of a unified power bloc, which was able to use its strong
position in parliament to counter the power of the monarchy. The
landed element in this power bloc was the dominant force in a
power elite which monopolized the levers of political power. When
industrialization took place, it did so within a firmly established
framework of landlord power. The continued salience of landowners
in political power was, in some respects, a characteristic feature of
all Europe in the nineteenth century. Despite the continual expansion of commerce, finance and manufacturing, the challenge to
landed power had been minimal. Landowners had, everywhere,
sought to offset opposition by offering opportunities of political
participation to members of the commercial and financial classes
and had sought to broaden their power blocs. As Mayer argues,

> Rather than yield institutional ground, they opted for this selective co-
> optation, confident of their ability to contain and defuse its attendant
> ideological and cultural contamination. This strategy or gamble paid
> off, for the fusion of the two strata remained manifestly asymmetrical:
> the aristocratization or nobilization of the obeisant bourgeoisie was
> far more pervasive than the bourgeoisification of the imperious
> nobility.[3]

The industrial revolution, of course, posed new strains on this
pattern of accommodation, and it is hardly surprising that Britain
should see the greatest strains on its old regime. Industrialization
in Britain was relatively early, and democratization was rather weak
in the absence of a revolutionary overthrow of the established power
elite. In France, by contrast, a democratic revolution was followed
by a relatively weak impulse to industrialization. Britain and France
constitute virtual polar types of the transition to modernity. Other
patterns of modernization vary between these two poles according
to the relative strength of industrialism and democracy, and the
relative lateness of their modernization.

In Britain, the long-standing interpenetration of land and financial
interests provided the basis for the formation of its particular power
bloc. British landowners were far more capitalistic in outlook than
were most of their European counterparts, and men of wealth had

always been able to enter the ranks of the gentlemen through the purchase of landed estates. As a result, industrialists acquired greater power in Britain than elsewhere, and the normative framework which legitimated their role was not the backward-looking ruralism of, for example, the German landowning class. Britain was also distinct in the degree to which the capitalist classes of land, finance and manufacturing were coming closer together in economic terms as a unified 'business class', though this was only fully formed in the inter-war years of the twentieth century.

The forces of modernity swept through Europe in the latter half of the eighteenth century, posing uncontainable strains on the *anciens régimes*. The impact of industrialism and democratization – the main expressions of modernity – were manifest in the emergence of a number of new words and of new 'modern' meanings for old words: industry, capitalism, class, bureaucracy, democracy, liberal, conservative, science, ideology, all acquired their modern meanings in this period. Perhaps the most obvious intellectual manifestation of this was the transformation of social thought and the emergence of sociology itself as an attempt to understand the evolving forms of social organization.[4] These conceptual innovations were indicators of the crucial importance of the long 'Victorian' period of the nineteenth century as the crucial pivot and point of transition between the old society and modern society.

The Old Society in England

How, then, can the structure of the old society in England be characterized? It can be seen as a society structured by the twin principles of *elitism*[5] and *patriarchy*. It was a hierarchical society which revolved around a group of 'gentlemen', predominantly landed, who justified their position as the leaders of society on the grounds of their 'natural' God-given authority. This dominant status group was also defined in terms exclusively of its male members, the dominance of the 'gentlemen'over women being firmly grounded in patriarchal principles.

The church played a key role in defining their status and in legitimating their cultural and political ascendancy. It legitimated the familial authority of the father, and these patriarchal attitudes permeated other social relationships: the clergyman was father to his congregation, the father of a family was father also to the servants of the household, the master was father to his apprentices

and workers, and so on. Patriarchy was expressed through a hierarchy of 'natural' authority for male heads of households.[6] Within
the public worlds of the state and the economy, access to formal
political power was structured by the relative status of the patriarchal
heads of households, and so a pattern was established within which
women had little or no part to play. In the private sphere of the
household itself, the senior male enjoyed ultimate power over all
other men, all women, and all children.

The dominant status group, the upper circle, and its political
power were rooted in the class structure of an agrarian capitalism.
But the old society was not an exclusively agrarian society. It was
a rural social order with provincial, urban enclaves and with its
commercial, financial and governmental activities focused on the
metropolis of London. The bulk of the members of the society,
however, depended upon the land as a source of income and of
livelihood. The landowners and farmers, and the numerous cottagers
and labourers, depended on it directly, while servants and village
craftsmen, and the various 'professionals' (the clergy, lawyers and
bankers) depended on it indirectly because of their role in servicing
landed society.[7]

Society was structured economically into distinct economic
locations, which were important determinants of life chances and
were the bases on which the social stratification of households was
built. At its simplest, as shown in figure 3.1, the economic locations
of the old society can be seen as structured into four separate levels,
reflecting the interplay of property ownership, managerial and manual skills, and labour power. At the upper levels were the major
landowners and financiers, rooted in the ownership and use of
substantial property and distinguished by the differing objects of
that property relation. Below them were a series of locations which
were involved with lesser amounts of property and whose occupants
were more directly involved in the use of this property on a day-
to-day basis. Next in the hierarchy came the craftworkers whose
property consisted exclusively of their workshop and their tools,
and whose advantages within the stratification system depended
rather more upon the manual skills which they could use to generate
an income. Finally, and accounting for the vast mass of the population, were labouring locations occupied by those whose sole marketable capacity was their labour power.

The middle orders of the rural stratification system comprised the
households of the 'parish gentry', petty absentee landowners and
yeomen farmers, who were the parliamentary electors and the hold-

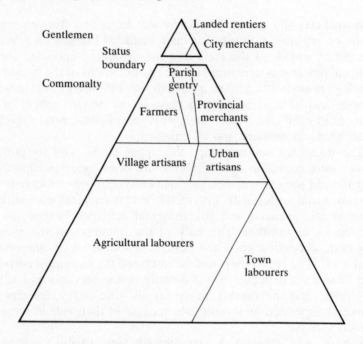

Figure 3.1   Economic locations in the old society

ers of the important parish offices. The landowning interests and influence of the parish gentry were limited to one or two villages, and they overlapped considerably with the smaller absentee land-owners who combined minor rural landholdings with commercial interests in the towns and cities. Yeomen farmers were, strictly, the owner-occupying farmers, though the term 'yeoman' was used rather loosely as a status designation, and the group cannot be easily distinguished from the more substantial tenant farmers who rented their land from the large and small landlords. These people – these *men* – were important forces in local affairs. They exercised considerable power over the families of the craftsmen and labourers who made up the bulk of the parish population, just as their urban counterparts dominated the populations of the towns. But the occupants of these 'middling' locations, in both town and country, were outside the ranks of the power elite of gentlemen.

The landed rentiers stood at the apex of the stratification system, and their economic base lay in their rental incomes from landhold-ings. These landholdings were run on capitalist lines, and the hold-ings of the capitalist landed class were segmented into large-scale

Plate 3.1 A Power House: Blenheim Palace, a gift from the government to the Duke of Marlborough to celebrate his victory of Louis XIV of France. (Reproduced by kind permission of A. F. Kersting.)

and small-scale capital. It has been estimated that there were about 400 large-scale 'magnate' landowners in the eighteenth century, together holding between 20 and 25 per cent of the total land. And there were anything up to 4,000 small scale 'county gentry' landowners, together holding between 50 and 60 per cent of the land.[8] The magnates generally had landholdings in more than one county, often in different regions, and they predominated in national politics. The county gentry, with landholdings limited to a single county, prevailed in local administration and the parliamentary representation of the county. While the magnates frequently held peerage titles, the county gentry generally made do with the customary title of 'squire'.

The class of landed rentiers was, I have argued, a capitalist class. They had adopted a market orientation towards their own land and the labour which they employed. Landownership and farming were subject to a continual process of 'improvement' in the attempt to raise returns and to increase efficiency. The eighteenth century was a period in which there was a strong drive towards the financial and technical concentration of landed capital: larger farms and larger estates were constructed by the magnates through enclosures and through land purchase.

Innovations in the techniques of farming were not, in general, sought or undertaken by the landowners as mere technical means to greater levels of production. As rentiers, they saw such matters as tasks to be undertaken by the farmers, along with the latter's responsibility for the management of stock and the marketing of produce. Landlords did, of course, encourage their tenant farmers to 'improve' the land, but their primary concern was to improve the prospects for the rents which they could charge. The consolidation of holdings through enclosure, for example, was actively promoted by large landowners because of the higher rents which could be earned from more compact and more efficient farms. The primary concern of the landed rentier was the financial returns which would accrue from improved farming.

The landowners' long involvement in sheep farming and wool production linked them closely to the cloth trade, and, hence, to the mercantile interests of the towns. During the eighteenth century, many of them became involved in mineral development and so acquired a wider range of business interests. Landowners invested in public funds and held money in bank deposits, many were involved in the financing of overseas trading ventures, and they had frequent recourse to lawyers and bankers to raise mortgages for new capital injections to their estates. Despite this strong commercial orientation, however, the landed class remained distinct from the urban monied class of merchants and financiers, and their capitalist outlook was contained within the normative framework of elitism and patriarchy which defined their relationship to the local communities and shaped their conception of the wider national society.

This normative framework was expressed in the attitude which was taken towards the family estate. The landed estate provided the material foundation for a family's continued existence, and its economic use was an integral part of a deliberate family strategy aimed at the reproduction of the family as a social and political unit. Family strategy was patterned by patriarchal attitudes which enjoined primogeniture and patrilineal descent, both necessary for the maintenance of the integrity of the 'house'. The house – the dynastic extended family household – was a term which was used to describe the family and its relationship to its property. The family name and titles, their residences and heirlooms, and, of course, their land were what defined the family as an established 'house'. It was the unity of all these elements which comprised the unity of the house.[9]

Patriarchy prescribed the passage of property to male descendants, following closely the main line of the family. Ideally, this involved inheritance by the eldest son of the current head of the house. In this way, an attempt was made to ensure that the family name, heraldic arms and any titles of nobility remained associated with the land. This was underlined by the inheritance of heirlooms – the deeds, wills and patents in the family archives, letters, portraits of ancestors, jewellery, furniture, and so forth, which made up the documentary and material record of the house. Genealogy was of central practical importance to the family, not only in legitimating descent and inheritance, but also in securing heirs when there was a failure in the male line. If a man was approaching death without a son to take over the family property, the family tree could be searched for distant cousins who might be in a position to inherit and maintain the integrity of the house. Only if this failed would female inheritance be considered. Inheritance of land through the female line was often associated with a requirement that the husband of the heiress change his name to that of the ancestral family line, or at least adopt a hyphenated, 'double-barrelled' surname. If the principal titles or arms were lost in this way, the family might petition the Crown for a new grant to bring land, name and title back together.

For all these reasons, the regulation of marriage was a central element in family strategy. Marriages were a family affair, rather than a purely individual matter. The integrity of the house was at stake, and so it was of considerable importance that 'appropriate' marriages were entered into and that all marriages were contractually regulated in such a way as to protect the interests of the family. Indeed, the drawing up of a marriage settlement for the heir was frequently used as an occasion to restructure the legal and financial affairs of the estate. This allowed the revenue and interests in the estate to be redistributed so as to provide for the needs of the various members of the family. Great care was taken to ensure, however, that these adjustments did not threaten the integrity of the house itself, and the contractual re-arrangements were not allowed to encroach on the core property of the family.

The core of a landed estate comprised the 'seat' itself and the principal lands – the residence and land most closely associated with the family history and family name. The wealthiest families owned numerous residences and held land in many parts of the country, and family strategy centred around a distinction between the *core* and the *peripheral* areas of the estate. The seat and the core lands of the estate were generally tied up in perpetuity, with only very limited opportunities for the current holder to sell or to mortgage it. The practice of the 'strict settlement' permitted the once-in-a-lifetime renegotiation of its terms on the marriage of an heir. This practice allowed the financial structure of the estate to be tidied up, but it did not permit any individual heir to alienate it completely.[10]

The peripheral areas of the large estates comprised smaller properties and land at the free disposal of the current owners. Peripheral lands and houses could be sold or mortgaged, and they could be added to when resources allowed this. It was through such adjustments in the peripheral areas that families sought to provide marriage portions for daughters and some degree of support for younger sons and other relatives. In this way, the association between the family of the oldest son and the core areas of the estate could be maintained.

Economically and politically, the old society was structured around the class of landed rentiers and the large capitalists of the cities, the latter having especially close business and personal relationships with the gentry. Together, these classes formed the power bloc of English society. In terms of status, however, the landed class and its values were supreme. The crucial status division was that between an upper circle of gentlemen and their families at the top and the 'common' people below; and the dividing line was drawn in such a way that only a *landed* gentleman could be a *real* gentleman. Other wealthy capitalists who sought acceptance in the dominant status system had to do so by buying into land to symbolize their acquiescence in the dominant values.

Until the seventeenth century, the magnate landowners had regarded themselves as a 'nobility', but the language of status was subtly transformed during the seventeenth and eighteenth centuries. As the magnates and gentry came together into a single class, and as the wealthier financiers and merchants achieved a greater degree of social recognition, the most important status division came to be seen as one between the 'gentle' and the commonalty rather than simply between the 'noble' and the rest of the population. 'Gentle', 'gentility' and 'gentleman' became the crucial terms for demarcating the upper circle of established social status from the common herd. By the eighteenth century the larger bankers, merchants, and lawyers had been assimilated into a dominant patrician status group of gentlemen, headed by the landed rentiers. It was this status group which comprised the power bloc of English society.

The patrician upper circle was separated from the rest of society by the sharp status division between the gentle and the common, but members of each group were tied to one another through vertical bonds of obligation. Within both the gentle and the common sections of society there were complex internal status gradations, and members of the various status levels were tied to one another through extensive chains of personal connections. Horizontal divisions of status were complemented by vertical bonds of patronage and support which tied people into networks of social obligation and deference. People were dependent on the help and support which others could provide, and this help often involved asking for additional help from someone further along the chain. To get positions in the civil service or jobs in domestic service, for example, meant asking a local influential person to intercede with those at a national level or in the 'big house' who might have the power to create such opportunities. Help provided meant an obligation incurred, and it was in this way that the vertical bonds of solidarity were built up.

The framework for these vertical chains of personal attachment was the system of property holding and the network of kinship and household connections. The chains followed the contours of property, employment and kinship and were commonly described in terms of 'friendship'. 'Friends' were those who were tied to one another through reciprocal personal obligations and dependence, including close relatives, wider kin, household servants and personal employees, tenants, political and business associates, and other connections and dependants. The chains of attachment further ramified through the relatives, household members, and employees of these people. For this reason, a 'friend' might frequently be very distant, unknown except through the requests and entreaties of one or more intermediary 'friends' (see box 3.1). Patrons were, in a patriarchal society, invariably men, though widows and mothers were not uncommon supplicants for patronage.

It was for this reason that the vertical bonds, though *personalized*, can be regarded as a rather formal feature of the social structure: activation of the personal bond of patronage required the use of formal requests and letter writing. Perkin has argued that

'Vertical friendship', a durable two-way relationship between patrons and clients permeating the whole of society, was a social nexus peculiar to the old society, less formal and inescapable than feudal homage, more personal and comprehensive than the contractual,

Box 3.1 *Views of patronage*

In 1792 Admiral Lord Nelson wrote about the son of a friend:

> You may rely that he shall be made [i.e., promoted] as soon after he has served his time as is in my power. The sons of brother officers have an undoubted claim to our protection and when to that is added the son of a very old friend, nothing my dear Lord can weigh stronger with me. Your conduct to *me* on 14 February [the Battle of Cape St. Vincent] has proved you a noble man.

But Admiral Lord Collingwood showed some reservations about his obligations. Writing in 1814 about someone that he had helped he said:

> he is 18 years old and as dull a lad as I ever saw. My conscience reproved me when I promoted him, which I made two or three attempts to do before I could bring myself to do it. Nothing but its being Admiral R's request could have induced me.

By the middle of the nineteenth century the demands of patronage were so great that the Duke of Wellington had (in 1841) special rejection slips printed:

> Field Marshal the Duke of Wellington presents his compliments. The Duke is Commander in Chief of the Army but he has no Patronage not exclusively Military, nor Countroul over those who have. He positively and distinctly declines to solicit favors for any Person whatever, but most particularly for a Gentleman of whom he knows nothing, not even whether or not he is trustworthy.

Sources: *Letters and Dispatches of Vice Admiral Lord Viscount Nelson*; M. Lewis, *Social History of the Navy* (1960); E. Longford, *Wellington: Pillar of State* (1969). I am grateful to Joe Banks and Christopher Dandeker for these references.

employment relationships of capitalist 'Cash Payment'. For those who lived within its embrace it was so much an integral part of the texture of life that they had no name for it save 'friendship'.[11]

This emphasis on friendship should not encourage the assumption that patronage necessarily involved care and consideration for subordinates. Even within the family itself such attitudes were far from universal. Patronage and personal obligation, actions involving the exercise of power and the pursuit of interest, were compatible with both coercion and constraint: 'Deference meant not mere servility; it involved sympathetic involvement, expectations of reciprocity, common outlook, identification of interest and sheer coercion in the name of a social ideal.'[12]

Particularistic relations among individuals were of primary importance in giving subjective meaning to a person's existence. This was a society in which all 'knew their place', but it was also a society in which one's 'place' was defined by a complex system of personal connections. These vertical chains of connection dimmed any consciousness of horizontal solidarity with those at the same status level. Only at the very top, amongst the gentlemen and their families, was there a strong horizontal sense of identity.[13]

The old society was a 'patrician state', headed as it was by a power bloc dominated by landed gentlemen who justified their authority on traditional elitist and patriarchal lines. The gentlemen were unified by their schooling, above all at such places as Westminster and Eton, which taught the tastes, manners, and morals of the patrician code. This power bloc was the origin of the norms and values of the cultural system that permeated the whole society. There was a widespread emulation of these upper-circle values at lower levels of the system, though this often involved a pragmatic accommodation rather than a moral acceptance.[14]

The state elite in eighteenth-century England was recruited from a power bloc which was dominated by a unified landed class. It had a power elite drawn from the highly restricted social background of the upper circle, a power elite with a high degree of cohesion and integration. Figure 3.2 sets out a model of the eighteenth-century polity through which this power elite operated. The Crown was not the all-important focus of political power that it had been in the seventeenth century, though 'the Crown in parliament' remained an important symbol of authority. The Hanoverian succession had put the final seal on the declining power of the monarchy, leaving the monarch – one of the wealthiest, if not *the* wealthiest, of the

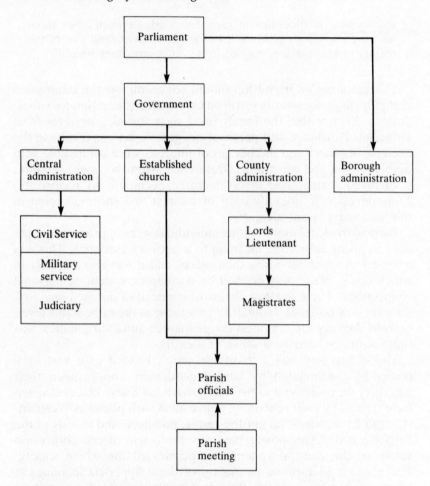

'Parliament', elected by county and borough voters, was the 'crown in parliament' and includes the role of the monarch. Boroughs and the City of London were self-governing, with a direct link to the crown.

Figure 3.2   The eighteenth-century polity

landed magnates – with merely residual powers of intervention in the political process. This is not to deny, of course, that the monarch could and did exercise real power. The point is that this power depended upon wealth and political influence: the monarch, in short, had to use the same mechanisms of political control as other landlords and could not rely on the formal institutional authority of the monarchy.

Plate 3.2 King George III: Country Gentleman. Painted by Thomas Gainsborough. (Copyright reserved to Her Majesty Queen Elizabeth II. Photograph: Rodney Todd-White and Son.)

Landlords had an almost complete control of parliament. The magnates dominated the Lords and they controlled a large number of borough seats in the Commons. The gentry and magnates together monopolized the representation of county seats in the Commons. Only in the Home Counties, around London, and in some of the provincial manufacturing areas did commercial interests achieve any direct parliamentary representation. Not until the 1760s did the number of merchants and lawyers in parliament show any significant increase.

Parliament was, in a very real sense, the foundation of government.[15] National government comprised the 'King's block' – the court and treasury interests – together with one or more magnate factions, the government generally being supported by enough 'independent' members to command a Commons majority. Shifting alliances of magnate factions were the basis of changes in 'party' government. Participation in the power elite was, in general, a direct reflection of landed and commercial property, actual involvement being shaped by the patronage and sponsorship of the magnates. These processes ensured a degree of 'openness', allowing some with little land or only limited wealth to become involved in politics. It was the rotten boroughs which were used for this purpose and which were, therefore, legitimated by the magnates as ways of bringing in men of talent and foresight who might not be elected in more open constituencies. In return for sponsoring the political careers of these people, the patrons, of course, expected to get their parliamentary support. In rare cases, the subtle use of contacts, setting one patron against another, could provide the basis of an 'independent' political career, though parliamentary independence was generally the prerogative of those of the landed gentry who were not beholden to a magnate.

The government appointed the leading members of the central and local administration. Its powers of appointment over bishops and archbishops in the Church of England made the established church, with its own legal and court system, a virtual branch of the state apparatus, reinforced by the participation of bishops in the House of Lords. Members of landowning families filled the top levels of the army and the navy, they occupied the judicial and magisterial benches, and they were the patrons whose influence could be used by those below them to secure junior positions in these same official hierarchies. The counties were self-perpetuating oligarchies of country gentlemen, meeting regularly as magistrates at Quarter Sessions and supervising parish administration, but the urban boroughs were independent enclaves of commercial power within the county territories. Boroughs operated through Royal Charter, but were constitutionally independent of the central state, electing and appointing their own mayors, aldermen, and councillors.

This, then, was the system of power within the old society of England. There was a power bloc composed of the landed and commercial classes and supported socially by an alliance of agrarian and propertied interests. This power bloc monopolized the leading positions of the state out of all proportion to its numbers. The capitalist landed class was a ruling class because it dominated the membership of the power elite and was able to ensure that the British state was operated in the interests of landed property.

The Transition to Modernity

Industrialization could not but have a disruptive effect on the structure of the old society. A whole new class of industrialists grew to massive proportions. As 'industry' began to undermine the economic primacy of land, so the industrial entrepreneurs began to challenge the political supremacy of the landlords. The emergence of a 'modern' society in Britain – the political union of England and Scotland had been consolidated by the end of the eighteenth century – was the birth of an 'industrial' society and of new class relations.

Economically, industrialization centred on the establishment of a factory system, with capital-intensive machinery, fragmentation of skills, and new forms of surveillance and labour discipline. The capitalist entrepreneur, the combined owner, manager and employer, was the major actor in the provincial districts where manufacturing became strongly established. Business connections were built between manufacturing entrepreneurs and the established commercial capitalists, and financial operations were themselves transformed through new forms of banking and stock dealing.

The vertical bonds of the old society were undermined by economic change and by the sheer growth in numbers. In an expanding society, claims upon patronage became all but unmanageable (see Box 3.1), and the old system of vertical solidarity began to break down. Economic locations became more important as markers of cultural and political divisions of interest and outlook. As the social significance of the old economic locations was transformed, so new locations were created. In commerce, and increasingly in manufacturing, whole armies of clerical and managerial employees were recruited to run the emerging bureaucratic forms of administration. Greater awareness of 'horizontally' structured mutual economic interests led people to identify with those in similar locations and so created sharply defined 'class' boundaries. Initially, the owners of manufacturing capital and the urban 'middling orders' of professional and clerical workers perceived themselves as closely linked together. They grew rapidly in numbers and in wealth alongside one another, and they shared common interests which were opposed to those associated with the leading elements of the old society.

From the turn of the nineteenth century, these people came increasingly to see themselves as a single class – as a 'middle class'. Despite their clear awareness of complex status gradations between upper middle class, lower middle class and just plain middle middle class, there was a perception of a common class position. This middle-class consciousness developed in opposition to the exclusionary practices of the landed gentlemen, who resented the rise of brash *nouveaux riches* and attempted to ignore their existence.

The landed gentlemen came increasingly to be seen as forming an 'upper class' distinct from the middle class. Though they might continue to see themselves as 'gentlemen', they were seen by others as an upper class. Further into the century, the outlook of the industrial workers housed in the expanding towns of the industrial north and midlands began to transcend the bounds of locality and trade and to take on a broader class nature. Manual workers in industry came to see themselves, and to be seen by others, as forming a 'working class'.[16] In the course of the nineteenth century, therefore, the social imagery of upper class, middle class, and working class became a feature of both informed social commentary and of political action.

The landed class, increasingly recognized by others as an 'upper class', began to reconceptualize their own standing and position. The word 'aristocracy' came into much wider use during the early years of the nineteenth century, its original Greek meaning of 'government by the best' being transformed into a status description of the upper circle as the source of the best possible governors of British society. The word glossed over the legal distinction between the peerage and the wider class of landowners, making it an especially useful term for emphasizing class unity. By virtue of their titles and their tendency to buy small country estates, the increasing number of ennobled financiers and merchants were easily assimilated under the same term. The word 'aristocracy' could, however,

serve at the same time to exclude the mass of capitalist manufacturers, who were merely 'middle class'. Thus, the language of class
came to use 'aristocracy' to describe the social category rooted in
the power bloc of the old society. The word 'gentleman' remained
in use to describe its individual members.

The 'middle-class' consciousness that emerged in this period
centred around what Perkin has called the 'entrepreneurial ideal'.[17]
This meaning system idealized the active owner-manager of an
industrial undertaking rather than the mere merchant. The entrepreneurial capitalist was the personification of capital as an active
economic force. He – very rarely she – was the motivating force of
the economic system. The key to legitimating the profits and power
of the capitalist was *competition*, as it was through competition that
the market – the impersonal arbiter of material success – was seen
to operate. Self-interested actions in a competitive market brought
about individual and collective benefit, and competition was also
seen as making 'self help' a possibility: a person with talent or merit
could, with sufficient energy, achieve success in the market. The
entrepreneurial ideal, therefore, ran counter to the principles of
patronage, the passive economic role of the rentier, and the pursuit
of leisure to which the aristocracy were committed. The new science
of political economy – the intellectual expression of the entrepreneurial ideal – sharpened middle-class consciousness with its
depiction of landownership as 'unproductive'.

The entrepreneurial ideal, therefore, was a mythical idealization
of certain features of the economic location of the entrepreneurial
capitalist. Entrepreneurs generally required some initial capital to
set up their undertakings, free competition was far from universal,
and there was no solid evidence that markets operated in the general
interest. Yet there was sufficient truth in the ideal for it to convince
most entrepreneurs and to appear as a highly plausible description
of the world to the expanding masses of the 'middle class'.

Social imagery in the Victorian period did not coincide with the
social differentiation by economic locations. In economic terms,
there were three capitalist classes: one based in land, one in finance
and commerce, and one in manufacturing industry. The first of
these saw itself as an aristocracy, and was grudgingly willing to
extend this recognition to the more prosperous and influential of
the financiers. 'Aristocracy' came to be a descriptive term for the
power bloc of the old society which sought to maintain its power in
the new society. The manufacturing capitalists saw themselves as
'middle class' and felt a unity of sorts with professional, managerial,

and clerical workers. As the manufacturing entrepreneurs began to challenge aristocratic power, 'middle class' came to designate what was, in effect, an alternative power bloc, one headed by the capitalist manufacturers who were excluded from a share in the exercise of state power.

The second half of the nineteenth century, therefore, was marked by the persistence of the old power bloc and the increasingly forceful challenge of a rival power bloc centred around the manufacturing capitalists. Each power bloc attempted to further its interests by gaining the support of the middle class and working-class masses. The industrialists sought to challenge the landed class by mobilizing popular support for 'reform', while the landowners responded by seeking popular support for a re-affirmation of traditional obligations and responsibilities.[18] The industrialists, however, did not push their challenge to the full. They were willing, as Marx recognized, to allow the patrician classes of 'Old England' to continue to exercise many of the powers of the central state on their behalf. Although increasing numbers of provincial manufacturers and merchants entered the state elite, they did little to challenge the existing power elite. Their political power was, however, much enhanced at the local level, as the entrepreneurs became the dominant force in the towns and cities that were pushing gentlemanly county administration into eclipse.

The political reforms of the 1830s and 1860s removed many of the techniques of electoral management which had been used in the old society. No longer able to rely on patronage and corruption, the power elite had to establish a new basis for its political rule, and the changing balance of power between classes was manifest in new modes of political representation. Industrial and 'middle-class' influence made itself felt in parliament through the introduction of the machinery of modern party politics. The new classes had formed a vast array of formal associations – Chambers of Commerce, campaign groups, and various 'leagues' and 'societies' – and the restructuring of the Conservative and Liberal parties as formal associations was testimony to the potency of this social innovation. An increasing reliance on vote-gathering in municipal elections had shown how similar mechanisms could be used to mobilize the constituency vote in an age of the competitive 'market' for public opinion which had been opened up by the enlarged parliamentary franchise.[19] The aristocratic power elite accommodated itself to the rising power of the class of industrialists by colonizing the emerging machinery of party politics. When party government became the norm, it did so under the aegis of the old aristocracy. In this way, the old and the new forces of capital began to merge.

The capitalist classes of land, commerce and industry moved closer towards one another, developing more and more areas of common concern and interest. The growing wealth of the industrialists, though still overshadowed by that of the landowners and commercial capitalists,[20] separated them more clearly from those in the middle classes who occupied petty bourgeois and service locations. By the end of the century, many industrialists had interests in land and in the City of London, and landowners were supplementing their declining incomes with their earnings from directorships in joint stock companies. The very rise of the joint stock company, of course, was an indicator that industrial capitalists were less 'entrepreneurial' and more 'rentier' in their business practices. There was the foundation for a unified capitalist business class with diversified rentier interests in land, commerce, and industry.

The final third of the nineteenth century saw the forging of a new power bloc. The industrialists found increasing acceptance by the aristocratic upper class, both groups perceiving common interests in the face of the threat posed by the great mass of the working class. The accommodation of interests between landowners, merchants, and industrialists led to the abandonment of some of their more radical ideas of popular mobilization. The new power bloc was created with the minimum necessary level of popular support. One strategy for countering the threat of mass participation in politics was to attract the support of the more reliable and 'respectable' sections of the working class in an electoral alliance which would buttress the continued dominance of the power bloc. Disraeli, for example, saw that the party machine could be used to defend the established social order through emphasizing common membership in 'One Nation'. The extended franchise, he argued, could be used as the basis of a stable electoral base for Conservative government: welfare reforms aimed at improving the 'condition of the people' would call forth a recognition of the 'natural' leadership qualities of the power elite.

The new power bloc consisted of landowners, financiers and industrialists, supported by the higher levels of the professional middle classes. At its core, and providing the membership of its power elite, was the group which came to be termed the 'establishment'. The men of great wealth comprised an exclusive upper circle of the status hierarchy, a group rooted in their common education in the reformed public schools and their commitment to the maintenance of the established traditions of old England. Most women still lacked the right to vote and, despite the Married Women's Property Act, there were few wealthy women able to enter the public sphere of politics. This 'establishment' dominated political power within the national and local state apparatus, and its power and influence stretched out to all the salient institutions of British society. The establishment was a tightly knit group of intermarried families which monopolized the exercise of political power in Britain.

Within this structure, however, landed property remained the touchstone for the status conventions and, thereby, the political power and influence of the whole power elite. In the period 1830–1868, between two thirds and three quarters of all M.P.s were from landed families; between one third and one quarter were manufacturers, merchants, or bankers. Over two thirds of cabinet members were landed. These groups did, however, have a similar social background – almost a half of all M.P.s in the period had attended a public school, with about a half of these being Harrovians or old Etonians.[21] The outlook of the establishment was an amalgam of the entrepreneurial ideal and the values of the old landed society. The primacy of land and the external trappings of the old society remained the dominant framework for political action, though these now permeated and circumscribed the new machinery of party politics. The landed class – for long a capitalist class – found it easy to accommodate to the money-making orientation of the industrialists, though its values accorded a superior cachet to second-generation industrial wealth and to those individuals whose fathers had sent them to a public school where they learned the values of a 'Christian gentleman'.[22]

In this chapter I have attempted to present an all too brief overview of the development of the British ruling class from the old society of the eighteenth century to the nineteenth-century transition to full modernity. It is now possible to use the ideas raised in chapters 1 and 2 in order to examine whether it is still appropriate to speak of a ruling class in twentieth-century Britain. In the following chapter I will explore the question of whether Britain still has a capitalist class; in chapter 5 I will ask whether the status hierarchy still has an upper circle; and in chapter 6 I will investigate whether there is still a ruling class.

4 Is there still a Capitalist Class?

Does Britain still have a capitalist class? There may be, in a purely statistical sense, a privileged class at the top of the class hierarchy, but the question is whether this is a capitalist class similar to those that existed in the eighteenth and nineteenth centuries: a privileged class rooted in a position of economic dominance in a capitalist system of production.

By the end of the nineteenth century it was clear that the creation of a unified propertied class, a class with complementary and inter-dependent interests in land, finance, and industry, was well under way. I shall argue that the merger of the contending capitalist classes of the nineteenth century continued during the present century and that, by the inter-war years, provincial industrialists, City merchants and financiers, and large landowners had finally merged to form a capitalist business class. This class, however, was rooted in forms of property ownership which differed markedly from those of their nineteenth-century predecessors.

I argued in Chapter 1 that a capitalist class owes its advantaged life chances to the specific economic locations which are occupied by its members. Capitalist-class households owe their position in the stratification system to the fact that one or more of their members occupies a capitalist economic location.[1] But what are the capitalist economic locations in the modern economy?

Capitalist economic locations involve participation in the structure of control and corporate rule in business. This participation may be immediate and direct, through personal property holdings in busi-ness enterprises, or it can involve administrative participation in the patterns of control through which business enterprises are ruled.[2] These locations are most clearly identifiable where direct personal ownership of capital exists, but they may also be found within the systems of 'impersonal' capital which have developed during the twentieth century.

The various writers discussed in Chapter 1 seemed to recognize that personal holdings had increasingly been replaced by the impersonal forms of joint stock enterprise, large-scale combinations, and institutional shareholdings. I shall argue that such structures and the economic locations which they define have become of ever increasing importance in the reproduction of the British capitalist class of today. This is the reason why research into the ownership and control of property is of such importance: the research enables us to map the transformation of property relations and so to understand the processes through which the capitalist business class is able to reproduce itself.

Who are the Capitalists?

Capitalist economic locations, I wish to argue, comprise positions within a structure of control over property, positions which are filled through specific patterns of recruitment and remuneration. A capitalist-class household is one whose advantages and life chances derive from the benefits which accrue from property and from involvement in the processes through which it is controlled. Max Weber described these advantages as being rooted in property and the commercial uses to which property is put.

Property holdings become the bases of personal income and wealth through the dividend and rental incomes which they generate. Personally owned controlling holdings in business units, whether in industry, in commerce, or in land, give property owners the power to be actively involved in determining the levels of these incomes from property. Their 'unearned income' from their property holdings depends directly on the abilities which they can bring to bear on the management of their property. This active relationship of the propertied with their property was the hallmark of the nineteenth-century capitalist entrepreneur, and it remains of major significance wherever such controlling interests in business units persist.

Managerialist writers saw the rise of the joint stock company as undermining personal property holdings through share dispersal and through the creation of bureaucratic hierarchies of corporate management. Those who served in the corporate bureaucracies, they argued, had replaced the capitalist entrepreneurs as the leading force in the modern economy. Even some writers who continue to be influenced by Marxist theory claim that the 'managers' comprise a 'service class' which has displaced the capitalist class.[3] It is important to recognize, however, that a decline in personal forms of control does not necessarily spell the decline of the capitalist class itself. Capitalist economic locations can persist alongside subordinate 'service' locations. Central to a capitalist location is the ability to ensure that property is used to one's sectional advantage. Those who merely 'serve' in the corporate bureaucracies are the servants of capital and, hence, of those who benefit from this capital. Those who benefit disproportionately and who are involved in the control over property – on whatever basis – are the occupants of capitalist locations.

This argument does not, of course, apply to all forms of property. Almost everybody has some kind of property – personal effects, consumer goods, cars, and houses – but most of this property is mere 'property for use'. It is consumed directly in order to provide improved living standards and is, in general, a depreciating asset. Cars and clothing, for example, rapidly lose their value. Houses are rather less likely to depreciate, and normally show a long-term appreciation in value. Nevertheless, a person's family home remains merely 'property for use', as its appreciating value cannot usually be realized: a home which is sold must normally be replaced with another if the person is not to become homeless.[4] The bulk of people's everyday property is irrelevant to the occupancy of capitalist economic locations.

Capitalist economic locations are defined by property which functions as capital, that is to say, in relation to various forms of 'property for power': property which gives control over the lives of other people.[5] This kind of property – shares, land, and other commercial assets – is typically an appreciating asset. It has a commercial use, which means that it both grows in value and generates an income. This enhanced value is readily realizable because the assets are marketable. Capitalist economic locations are rooted in particular forms of 'property for power'.

The qualification 'particular forms' is important, as small-scale capital must be distinguished from its large-scale counterpart. Although small-scale capital may sometimes offer high personal rewards, entry to true capitalist locations is neither easy nor frequent from these 'petty bourgeois' locations. True capitalist locations, the basis of a capitalist class, are to be found only in the sphere of large-scale capital. Giant business enterprises, large landed estates, and massive share portfolios are the foundations of the capitalist class.

Figure 4.1 sets out a typology of capitalist economic locations, using two dimensions: the *nature* of a person's involvement in units of capital and the *number* of units in which there is an involvement. Participation in the control and rule of units of capital may follow from personal property ownership or from the occupancy of a directorship. The pure cases of involvement through property ownership occur where business activity is direct and unmediated by such legal forms as those of the joint stock company. In such circumstances, capitalist locations rest upon active involvements or passive benefits in personally owned and controlled units of capital. Once business enterprise comes to be organized through the joint stock company, people can achieve positions of power and influence through their occupancy of a directorship. The limiting case of involvement through a directorship is where the director holds no personal shareholding in the enterprise which he or she directs but is a mere occupant of a ruling position in a system of impersonal capital. The question of the number of units of capital in which people are involved is important, as it influences the character of a person's involvement. Those involved in a single unit of capital, for example, can give it their full attention, while those involved in many units must divide their time among them. Single and multiple involvements, therefore, require different mechanisms of action.

Cross-classifying these two dimensions gives the four categories of figure 4.1. The *entrepreneurial capitalist* is one whose involvement

Nature of involvement

No of involvements	Property ownership	Directorship
Single	Entrepreneurial capitalist	Executive capitalist
Multiple	Rentier capitalist	Finance capitalist

Figure 4.1   Capitalist economic locations

in business is distinguishable from the existence of a joint stock company and its system of directorships. The entrepreneurial capitalist exercises direct and immediate control over all aspects of business operations, and the ideal type corresponds to the image of the entrepreneur in classical economics and in classical Marxism. The *rentier capitalist* is one who has personal investments in a number of units of capital through direct-ownership stakes, membership of partnerships and trusts, or shareholdings. The orientation of the rentier capitalist is passive, by contrast to the active involvement of the entrepreneurial capitalist, and the ideal type corresponds to the image of the 'dividend recipient' and 'coupon clipper' in Marxism and Fabian theory. The *executive capitalist* is involved exclusively as an office holder in a joint stock company. In the limiting case, the executive capitalist is propertyless and dependent purely on the remuneration of office, corresponding to the managerialist image of the business leader in the modern corporation. The *finance capitalist* is also, in the limiting case, propertyless, but occupies directorships in numerous units of capital. While the executive capitalist is one who plays a full-time bureaucratic role, the finance capitalist spreads his or her involvements by acting as a part-time 'outside' or 'non-executive' director. By virtue of involvement in a number of separate units of capital, the ideal type of the finance capitalist corresponds to the image depicted in Marxist theory.

As ideal types, of course, these categories cannot be applied directly to the situation in any particular society. They are tools for understanding the capitalist locations of modern capitalism as approximations to ideal types. The entrepreneurial capitalists of modern capitalism, for example, are often the holders of majority or minority shareholding stakes in joint stock companies and are also involved as directors of their companies. Their directorships are consequences of and means for the exercise of the powers attached to their personal property.

The rise of the joint stock company transformed the relationship between individual property holders and the businesses in which their property functioned as capital. The capitalist entrepreneur ceased to be the immediate owner of the undertaking, becoming a shareholder in a company which, in turn, owned the business assets. By adopting the joint stock form, entrepreneurs could draw on the funds of other individuals, who also became shareholders in the company. This led to a differentiation between the active shareholder – the capitalist entrepreneur – and the mass of passive shareholders who provided the capital and received the dividends but who played no active part in running the business. But not all shareholders are powerless; they are not all excluded from control. While the owner of a few pounds in shares in a large enterprise cannot be regarded as having any significant say in its affairs, the owner of a majority of the shares has a power to determine the outcome of all its decision-making processes. Despite the fact that large numbers of shares are held by a myriad of small shareholders, the owner of the majority stake has effective control of the business. Similarly, a large minority holding may be enough to ensure a working control of the company. The entrepreneurial capitalist of the twentieth century is one who holds a majority or a substantial minority of the shares in a company.[6]

But the joint stock company did not simply lead to a differentiation between the entrepreneurial capitalist and the mass of small shareholders. It also transformed the position of the rentier capitalist. Rentier capitalists had long been important sources of share capital for the large-scale joint stock companies in banking, insurance, and railways, but with the expansion of joint stock enterprise in industry their numbers and their significance were greatly increased. They became shareholders with substantial but non-controlling interests in large companies, shareholders whose holdings form parts of diversified portfolios of investments. Although their life chances are determined by their personal property, they are not entrepreneurs: they are uninvolved in the day-to-day running of the undertakings in which they invest. The typical rentier capitalist adopts an 'absentee' stance towards property. The rentier's interest lies merely in the income which the property generates and its impact on his or her wealth. Though passive with respect to the actual operations of the enterprises in which they invest, however, the rentiers are necessarily involved in the management of the property itself. A substantial portfolio of investments and other assets must be carefully stewarded if it is to generate an optimum income – the rentier must pay attention to the spread of investments, their relative yields, and the incidence of taxation. Even when portfolio management is partially delegated to professional advisers, rentier capitalists have a continuing personal involvement in the management of his or her property holding.

Where controlling holdings are held by financial institutions and corporate interests, rather than by particular individuals and families, property and control over property have become 'depersonalized'. In such a situation of impersonal property, the powers of corporate rule are exercised by boards of directors whose members have, at most, only small shareholdings in the enterprises which they direct. Although their personal shareholdings may be, and often are, extremely valuable in monetary terms, they amount to insignificant fractions of the total capital of the businesses and provide no basis for personal control of an entrepreneurial kind. Rather, the boards of directors function *collectively* as capitalists, their powers of corporate rule being dependent upon the impersonal structure of corporate and institutional shareholding.[7]

The executive capitalist is the director of a single unit of capital, while the finance capitalist is a 'multiple director' sitting on the boards of a number of companies.[8] The executive capitalist is typically a full-time official of an enterprise, occupying a post at the heart of its system of rule. Many of the most important will hold office as 'Chief Executive', 'Managing Director', or, in the United States, 'President', but there is also a wide range of executive titles corresponding to particular business roles. Executive capitalists stand at the heads of the corporate bureaucracies which are filled by those in service locations, and the typical executive capitalist is one who has risen from a service location relatively late in his or her career. For this reason, the executive capitalist location is a relatively insecure basis for membership in the capitalist class. A person who occupies a capitalist location for the whole of their life has a considerably greater chance of enjoying the advantages of a privileged life style and of passing them on to their children. The late entrant to an executive capitalist location may earn a large enough income to enjoy this life style for a period, but only the most highly paid and most financially astute will be able to continue to enjoy them after retirement.

The growth of institutional shareholdings led to the development of a system of 'finance capital', a system of capital mobilization in which industry and finance were fused.[9] Within this system, the fusion of enterprises at board level led to the emergence of an 'inner circle' of company directors who function as finance capitalists. Occupants of these locations have insignificant personal stakes in the enterprises of which they are directors, but they have accumulated large numbers of directorships and represent the interests of the controlling institutions on the boards of the controlled companies. The typical finance capitalist holds non-executive directorships and depends not on high earnings from a particular enterprise but on the accumulation of fees from numerous directorships. While the executive capitalist is centrally involved in the collective rule of a particular unit of capital, the finance capitalists play a part in the coordination and cohesion of numerous separate enterprises. Their interests are not limited to one particular company, but extend to whole industries or to the economy as a whole.

The ideal typical locations defined in Figure 4.1 are, in Weber's terms, locations among which mobility is both easy and frequent, and particular individuals may occupy a number of locations simultaneously. Rentier capitalists, for example, were well-placed for recruitment to the boards of companies which came under institutional control during the 1930s, and as the shareholding institutions sought to cement their growing links with industrial companies, the rentiers were important recruits to these boards as well. Thus, many finance capitalists were – and are – also rentier capitalists with extensive personal interests in the success of the capitalist system as a whole.[10] Similarly, entrepreneurial capitalists, as their interests in their own companies decline, become attractive recruits to the ranks of the finance capitalists, and may also diversify their holdings to adopt a rentier stance towards the system of property. Many top salaried executives who lack a propertied background are able to achieve entry to the ranks of the finance capitalists. Executive entrants, however, are in an insecure position unless they are able to convert their high incomes into property holdings and enter the ranks of the rentiers. The categories of capitalist economic locations, therefore, overlap considerably in concrete situations.

Although I have described the various capitalist economic locations in terms of the structure of industrial and financial enterprises, it must not be assumed that they relate only to these. During the course of the twentieth century the patterns of control and use in landed property, which were formerly distinct from those in such areas as manufacturing and banking, have become increasingly assimilated to other forms of capitalist enterprise. Landed estates and farms today can be understood in the same terms as any other units of capital.

The agricultural depression of the last third of the nineteenth century forced many of the old landed rentiers to reduce their landholdings through the sale of the more peripheral parts of their estates. This tendency was reinforced during the present century by fiscal challenges to inheritance and by the social changes which followed the First World War. Land sales boosted the numbers of owner-occupier farmers, many of whom became increasingly important as owners of extensive tracts of landed property. As a result, the ranks of the farmers became more sharply differentiated into those with large-scale and those with small-scale undertakings. Large estates and large farms, therefore, joined large enterprises, despite their varying legal forms, as the bases of essentially similar capitalist economic locations.[11]

The absentee landowner and the resident landowner are the descendants – often genealogically as well as economically – of the landowners of the old society. The absentee who owns land in various parts of the country is analogous to the rentier who owns shares in a number of companies, while the resident landowner with a single, compact estate adopts a role similar to that of the entrepreneur. Between these two categories are to be found the occupants of capitalist locations which combine features of both the rentier and the entrepreneurial role in land ownership. In farming businesses, the owners of large farms – both the 'gentleman farmers' and the more 'traditional' farmers – are entrepreneurial capitalists, involved in the active management of their undertakings, and like their industrial counterparts they are distinguishable from the small farmers of the entrepreneurial middle class.

It is not, of course, only individuals and families which own and farm land. The greater involvement of industrial and commercial enterprises in the management of urban and industrial land has been matched by the formation of farming companies whose forms of ownership are the same as those in other sectors of the economy. Specialist firms in food production have bought farms and transformed themselves into vast 'agribusinesses', whose shares have been acquired by insurance and investment companies. These same institutions have become even more closely involved with the land by providing funds to personal landowners and by acquiring farms and estates for themselves. As a result, the interests and involvements of the executive and finance capitalists have spread from industry and banking into farming and land.[12] Land is no longer a completely separate and distinct economic category; it has become more closely fused with activities in other sectors of the economy. Many landowners who have inherited their estates through a long family line have 'opened to the public' and built such attractions as fun fairs, motor museums, and safari parks. Country houses – whether owned by 'traditional' landowners or by 'newcomers' who have made money in other sectors of the economy – have been converted into hotels and conference centres, closely integrated with capital invested in hotels and leisure enterprises.

It is very rarely the case today that a particular capitalist-class household owes its life chances exclusively to its members' occupancy of a particular economic location or to involvement in a narrow sector of the economy. The boundaries between rentiers and entrepreneurs, executives and finance capitalists are blurred by the overlap and mobility which exists among the occupants of these locations. For this reason, neither the typology of locations nor the distinction between land ownership and other forms of property ownership should be seen as defining distinct *class segments*.[13] Such economic differentiation as does exist is not generally associated with a parallel social and cultural differentiation into separate groups with divergent interests. While it is possible to recognize some persisting separation of industrial entrepreneurs, 'traditional' land-owners, and corporate executives, for example, the vast bulk of capitalist class households are unified in both interests and outlook.

Capitalist economic locations, therefore, comprise those of the rentier, the entrepreneur, the executive, and the finance capitalist. In land, commerce, finance, and industry, large-scale undertakings are controlled and ruled by the occupants of these locations, operating through systems of personal and impersonal possession. The capitalist business class of Britain today consists of those whose family wealth and life chances are generated by the involvement of their members in these capitalist economic locations.

The Development of the Business Class

I have claimed that changes in the structure of property and of investment have led to fundamental transformations of the capitalist economic locations which had developed during the nineteenth century. These changes in the pattern of ownership and control were associated with a spatial restructuring of the British economy and of its emerging capitalist business class. During the nineteenth century the economy had been strongly structured along regional lines. The spatial distribution of industries was shaped by the distribution of natural resources, by the limited extent of the markets in which firms operated, and by the tendency of firms to rely on local sources of investment funding. The myriad local banks of the eighteenth century had been welded into a number of regional chains through mergers, and these chains became the foci of much regional economic activity. Distinct regional economies could be found in Scotland, the north east of England, the north west, the midlands, south Wales, and elsewhere. In each of these parts of the country a regional structuring of economic activity was the basis of regional industrial and commercial dynasties, which became closely allied with the county landowners in their region.

As companies grew in scale and shifted their operations from the local level to the larger national and international markets, their capital needs had increasingly to be met through the stock exchange. Controlling families were frequently unable to provide all the capital required, and they formed joint stock companies to draw on the wider pool of capital available through the City of London. Wealthy families were able to diversify their property holdings through the stock market and the banking system and so could move from entrepreneurial to rentier locations. The restructuring of the British economy into an integrated national economy weakened the attachments of the regional dynasties to their localities as they entered into stronger business connections with those in other parts of the country. The unified capitalist business class that developed in the course of the present century was formed on a regional basis, but the integration of the regional business dynasties meant that the class lost many of the regional features which had characterized its predecessors.[14]

These processes can be illustrated from the development and transformation of business dynasties in one particular region, the north east of England.[15] The original economic bases of the north-eastern business dynasties were in the eighteenth-century coal, glass, iron, and lead industries. These industries were, for the most part, organized and financed by local merchants and landowners. Many of the successful families were subsequently able to diversify into the newly developing industries of the nineteenth century. During the second half of the century, engineering and shipbuilding became the leading industries of the region, and the established industrialists became its leading entrepreneurs and financiers. They became the dominant forces in the local railway, water, and gas companies; they were involved in overseas ventures in mining, rubber, metals, and ranching, and they also entered the new electricity and tramway businesses. The regional system of capital mobilization ensured the smooth transfer of surplus funds from one type of venture to another. Regional banks and investment companies, linked to a regional stock exchange, were the channels through which additional funds could be made available to regional industrialists. Industry and land were closely connected. A number of the industrial entrepreneurs came from a landed background, and those who did not tended to purchase small estates. It was on this basis that, by the turn of the twentieth century, a relatively small group of capitalist families held control of an expanding pool of capital operating in many different sectors of the local economy.

Those families who lived in the city of Newcastle itself were congregated in certain districts, above all in Benwell and the wider West End. They were involved with one another in the Northern Counties Club, the Union Club, and the Literary and Philosophical Society, and they were involved in local politics through the new County Councils and the magisterial bench. Members of the business dynasties represented local interests in parliament, and some rose to national prominence. Sir Matthew Ridley, later Lord Ridley, for example, was Home Secretary from 1895 to 1900.[16] There was, by the time of the First World War, a strong regional business clique, a local capitalist class.

The leading members of this business system in north-eastern England were the Cookson and Pease families. The Cooksons were originally merchants and became the dominant force in the lead industry. From this base they moved into collieries, iron works, glass manufacturing, and banking. The foundation of the Pease family wealth was in the Yorkshire woollen industry, from where they established coal and iron interests in Teeside. This, in turn, became the base for their entrance into local banking and into the financing of Stephenson's locomotive works and the Stockton and Darlington railway.

Together with the Ridley, Joicey, Priestman, Straker, and Armstrong families, the Cooksons and Peases formed the core of a network of local dynasties. Financial links between families, arising from their common involvement in business enterprises, were complemented by kinship links and extensive networks of intermarriage were formed. Each family was able to draw on its kin, friends, and associates to construct the partnerships which would finance its growing business activities. As joint stock companies became a more important element in business operations, the intersecting partnerships among the various families were transformed into interweaving shareholdings and interlocking directorships. The close links of technical cooperation and integration to which these led were often a prelude to the amalgamation of enterprises and the restructuring of their ownership and control during the early years of the century.

Heavy industry was particularly badly hit by the depression of the 1930s, and the response of the north-eastern business dynasties was to form tighter combines and cartels in order to try to protect their industrial interests. Many of these groupings were organized on a regional basis, but it became increasingly important to obtain the financial support of the large national banks and insurance companies of the City of London. Indeed, the national banking chains had been formed through the merging of regional banks with those in London. The formerly independent regional banks became mere branches of national chains, with limited decision-making autonomy. As a result, many financial and investment decisions were removed from the regional level. Although local families retained majority or minority control of many industrial enterprises, some of these firms passed, through amalgamation, out of local control and into large national combines. At the same time, there were important shifts in the behaviour of the middle-class savers and investors who made up the mass of small, passive shareholders. These people were increasingly attracted to 'indirect' forms of company investment such as investment and unit trusts, and there was a massive growth in insurance business. These financial institutions, therefore, came to control large amounts of capital, which they invested through the stock exchange. Shareholdings by the original controlling families of the large enterprises of the north east became proportionately smaller as their companies grew in size, and their holdings were supplemented by the holdings of other wealthy families and of financial institutions.

While seeking to protect their interests in local industries, the north-eastern families also sought to protect their wealth by diverting their companies and funds into new areas. Some families reduced their holdings in the firms with which they had long been associated and built up more diversified investment portfolios, and many local firms were diversified into completely new areas. A particularly striking example of this diversification was the conversion of the local electricity companies into general investment and holding companies. This was hastened by the post-war nationalization of the coal and power industries, which finally freed local families from their dependence on declining regionally based heavy industry and gave them considerable capital for re-investment. With this boost to their diversified investment portfolios, the regional entrepreneurs had become nationally-orientated rentier capitalists.

A considerable number of the north-eastern families remained active in business as directors of regional and national enterprises. Locally, they built up a greater participation in building societies, property and investment, insurance, and commercial distribution. At the national level, they had a wide spread of interests: the Pease, Noble and Ridley families, for example, were all represented on the board of Lloyd's Bank, the Pease and Clayton families were on the Barclays board, and the Ridleys were on the National Provincial. The families became a part of the City of London business clique and were very active in representing its interests through their seats on the boards of industrial concerns. The north-eastern rentiers had become a major pool of recruitment for the finance capitalists who manned the national system of finance capital.

In the post-war period, the north-eastern families retained many links with the region which their ancestors had dominated, though few of them then lived in the urban area of Newcastle itself. Their business and civic involvements had also changed in character. Formerly they had run the politics of the region and had represented it in national decision-making forums. After the middle of the century, this relationship between the regional and the national level was reversed. Members of the business dynasties were more frequently coopted on to national and central state agencies in order to represent their interests within the region. This was, for example, the nature of their participation in the Federation of British Industry, later the Confederation of British Industry, in other employers' organizations, the Northern Industrial Development Board, and the Development Corporations for the new towns at Peterlee, Newton Aycliffe, Washington, and Cramlington. The purely regional connections which they retained became of less significance to their lives and those of others living in the region.

At the national level, it is possible to document the rise of the rentier capitalists as a significant force in industry and finance from the latter half of the nineteenth century. The rentier capitalists grew in numbers along with the joint stock companies, but they became a particularly important element in company finance with the drive towards amalgamation and merger which began around the turn of the century. When family-controlled enterprises merged with one another in order to achieve technical and financial economies, the holdings of each individual family were diluted. Ten families which each owned 100 per cent of their small family concerns, for example, might each expect to own only 10 per cent of the large holding company formed to take over their businesses.

Many of these families had, in fact, already diluted their controlling stakes to well below 100 per cent, and there were frequently many more than ten companies involved in the turn-of-the-century mergers. As a result, family holdings in the enlarged enterprises were often very small in percentage terms, and a substantial pool of rentier families were produced. In the absence of a single controlling entrepreneurial shareholder, the rentier families with an interest in a particular company would vie with one another for positions on the board in order to continue to participate actively in the control of their capital. As these companies grew in size during the course of the century the rentier holdings were further reduced in percentage terms, though ever increasing in monetary value. Families were able to spread their risks by investing in a large number of separate companies, and it was less important to be involved in the active management of any one of these interests. As they diversified their investments, the rentiers became a major element in stock exchange finance by the inter-war years.

Rentiers and entrepreneurs became the dominant forces in company shareholding, but they were supported by a growing number of 'institutional' shareholders which managed the savings of the wider population. Banks and insurance companies invested their funds in large companies and buttressed the powers of entrepreneurs and rentiers. Members of rentier families were recruited as directors of the very institutions which sustained their advantages by managing much of their capital. In this way, many were imperceptibly transformed into finance capitalists.

Since the 1930s, the financial power of the investing institutions has increased considerably. Concentration of economic activity in the hands of ever smaller numbers of large companies has gone hand-in-hand with the acquisition of larger numbers of shares by financial institutions. Entrepreneurial capitalists have remained an important element in the system of large-scale capital, albeit with majority or minority holdings rather than full ownership, and their role has been especially significant in such industries as retailing, property, and the manufacture of food and drink, but they have increasingly had to accommodate themselves to the financial institutions which have taken large shareholdings in their companies. Although those entrepreneurs who hold a majority of the shares in their companies remain very secure in their control, smaller minority stakes have become less secure bases of entrepreneurial control, and entrepreneurs have often come to depend on the support and acquiescence of financial institutions.

The significance of institutional ownership can be seen very clearly in table 4.1, which shows the forms of control in large enterprises in 1988. Seventeen of the top 50 financials and 96 of the top 200 non-financials – almost a half of the top 250 enterprises – were controlled by institutions. In these companies, there was no single shareholder or group of associated shareholders with sufficient

Table 4.1 *Control of large companies (1988)*

| | Top 250 companies of 1988 (no.) | | |
	Industrial	Financial	Total
Controlled by entrepreneurs	21	6	27
Controlled by institutions	96	17	113
Foreign, state, & other control	83	27	110
Totals	200	50	250

Source: Calculated from data collected for J. Scott, 'Corporate Control and Corporate Rule: Britain in an International Perspective', *British Journal of Sociology*, 41 (1990).

shares to determine the affairs of the enterprise. The shares were, in each case, widely dispersed, but the degree of dispersal was not of the kind depicted by proponents of the managerial revolution. The bulk of the shares were held not by an anonymous mass of small shareholderes but by vigorous and well-informed institutions: banks, insurance companies, pensions funds, and investment groups. The ownership of these companies was part of a system of impersonal property, and their mode of control has been described as control through a constellation of interests. The largest shareholders, almost all of them financial institutions, hold sufficient shares in aggregate in each company to exercise a real and effective constraint over the directors and managers. But the blocks of dominant shareholders in each particular enterprise do not comprise tight controlling groups: they have certain general interests in common, but they are beset by rivalries and competitive sectional interests.[17]

The boards of the companies which are controlled through constellations of interests are filled by executive capitalists and finance capitalists, the latter sitting on two or more boards and, in the great majority of cases, holding directorships in both the financial and the non-financial sectors. The integration of finance, commerce, and industry through the interweaving shareholdings of the large institutions is paralleled by the interlocking directorships of the finance capitalists who represent institutional interests on company boards. The finance capitalists constitute what Useem has described as an 'inner circle' of coordinating directors who can act as the collective voice of capital.[18] The size of the inner circle depends upon how many enterprises are included within the category 'very large'. If the top 250 enterprises are taken as a reasonable basis for assessment, they will be found to number fewer than 300. In 1976, for example, there were 282 men and no women with two or more directorships in companies in the top 250 industrial and financial enterprises. In 1988 there were 290 multiple directors on the boards of the top 250 companies, five of these people being women. Over two thirds of these leading finance capitalists held a directorship on a bank or insurance company, and a half of these were bank or insurance executives. Through their directorships, they tied the financial institutions into an extensive network which extended to include the major industrial and commercial enterprises. The institutions are hegemonic in the mobilization of capital, and the members of the inner circle represent the interests of the hegemonic institutions on the various boards of which they are members.

Table 4.1 also shows that there remained 27 of the largest companies with entrepreneurial controllers, and the names of the very largest are shown in table 4.2. Entrepreneurial control, through either majority or minority holdings, was especially strong in retailing, food and drink, hotels and leisure, and in merchant banking.[19] In these companies the entrepreneurial capitalists who occupied the roles of chairman of the board or chief executive had considerable power to determine corporate affairs. Many of these people were members of families which combined their entrepren-

Table 4.2 *Control of very large companies (1988)*

	Non-financial	Banking	Insurance
Institutional control	Shell Transp. & Trading, BAT Industries, ICI, British Gas, Unilever	Nat. Westminster, Barclays, Lloyds, TSB Group	Prudential, Legal & General, Commercial Union, Sun Alliance, Guardian Royal
Entrepreneurial control	S. & W. Berisford, J. Sainsbury, George Weston, Lonrho, Sears Holdings	Kleinwort Benson Lonsdale, Robert Fleming Holdings, Schroders, N. M. Rothschild, Barings	

Source: As table 4.1.

eurial stance with a rentier orientation towards other enterprises – they had diversified investment portfolios and extensive corporate interests.

Those enterprises which are controlled neither by entrepreneurs nor by institutions are significant in number, and they include those which were controlled by foreign multinationals and by the state.[20] Foreign ownership was the largest sector, with American multinationals playing a particularly important role. Although the state sector of the economy shrunk during the Thatcher years through a policy of economic 'privatization', there were still 12 very large state-controlled enterprises among the top 250 of 1988 – these included such giants as British Telecommunications, the Electricity Council, British Coal, British Steel, and British Petroleum. Whether through substantial shareholdings or through the form of a nationalized 'public corporation', branches of the state apparatus were responsible for the appointment of directors to these enterprises and for determining their broad policies. The slight shrinkage of the state sector in the Thatcher years has been interestingly paralleled by an increase in the extent of foreign ownership – there were 28 foreign-controlled companies in the top 200 non-financials of 1976, but 40 in the top 200 of 1988. The British economy had experienced a significant internationalization over the period.

Contours of the Capitalist Class

Having reviewed the development of the capitalist class during the twentieth century, it is time to try to assess the size of the class and to estimate its advantages and privileges relative to the rest of the population. Estimates of the distribution of income and wealth are notoriously difficult to make and to interpret, but I shall attempt to highlight the salient conclusions from recent research.

The richest families of the late nineteenth century were those of the great landowners – above all, the families of the Dukes of Sutherland, Westminster, Devonshire, Portland, and Bedford, with some of the other great peerage families such as the Stanleys (the Earls of Derby).[21] There were also, however, the wealthier financial and commercial families of the City of London and of the great commercial centres of Liverpool and Glasgow, together with a few wealthy families with their roots in the manufacturing districts of Lancashire and the midlands. The closer merger of industry, commerce, and land into a unified capitalist class had become more marked by the First World War, and this was a time when the great plutocratic business dynasties had achieved an unprecedented public visibility. There were Rothschild, Baring, Schroeder, and de Stern in banking, Guinness, Charrington, Allsopp, and Bass in brewing, Lord Leverhulme, the Tennants, Brunners, and Monds in chemicals, Lords Rhondda and Joicey and the Weirs in coal and iron, Cayzer, Runciman, Currie and Ellerman in shipping, Coats in textiles, Wills in tobacco, the South African fortunes of Wernher and Beit, and many others.

This capitalist class stood at the head of a highly inegalitarian structure of income and wealth. The top 1 per cent of the population at the time of the First World War held more than a half of the country's total wealth. During the inter-war years the massive income inequalities of Victorian and Edwardian England began to decline, and there was a substantial reduction in the number and size of the great plutocratic incomes of landowners and industrialists alike. Capitalist incomes from land and the old industries fell, and income tax became a more significant redistributive force. The trend towards less income inequality continued into the post-war period, with the Second World War and the 1945 Labour government putting the seal on a fundamental shift in welfare and redistribution policy. The top 1 per cent of income earners received 11 per cent of all personal income in 1949, but only 5 per cent in 1976. After taking into account the effects of taxation, the top 1 per cent of 1976 received just 4 per cent of total personal income. There is, however, growing evidence that since the late 1970s – some date it from the Conservative election success of 1979 – there has been a reversal of this trend, as taxes have been reduced and higher earnings encouraged.[22]

A similar, though less marked, decline in the inequality of wealth has taken place since the First World War, and this trend was, again, more marked in the period since the Second World War. The top 1 per cent of wealth holders in 1936 had 53 per cent of wealth, but only 27 per cent in 1973. An estimate for 1986 suggests that the share of the top 1 per cent had fallen to 21 per cent.[23] A major cause of this decline in inequality has been the growth of home ownership, which has increased the wealth of the less wealthy relative to that of the rich. The easier availability of mortgages, through the expanding financial institutions, has meant that increasing middle-class and working-class incomes have been the basis for an increase in their wealth. Clearly, however, housing – as 'property for use' – is not truly realizable or liquid wealth for its current holders, money and 'property for power' as sources of wealth remain highly concentrated. Although shares have become more widely distributed through the privatization of state assets – the percentage of the adult population owning shares increased from 6 per cent in 1984 to 20 per cent in 1988 – this has not led to an increase in the number of *large* personal shareholdings. Substantial shareholdings remain tightly concentrated.

To talk simply of the top 1 per cent, however, is misleading. The top 1 per cent of the population may be those who are 'privileged' – the especially affluent – but this is a much wider group than the capitalist class. The top 1 per cent includes not only the capitalist business class, but also many members of the professions and management who are more appropriately seen as members of the service class. The capitalist class is a considerably smaller group than the top 1 per cent, and the extent to which its income and wealth has followed these same trends is uncertain. It is likely that the trend towards greater equality has had a greater impact on the upper middle class than it has had on the capitalist class itself.

The core of the capitalist business class comprises about 0.1 per cent of the adult population, about 43,500 people, and it has been estimated that these people held 7 per cent of total wealth in 1986. That is to say, this small group which makes up one tenth of the top 1 per cent of wealth holders has one third of all the wealth owned by the top 1 per cent. Wealth becomes more highly concentrated at the very top of the hierarchy. This small group of 43,500 adults each held, in 1986, at least £740,000 in bank deposits, shares, land, and other forms of property. About two fifths of their wealth was held in the form of company shares, and about one third consisted of land, buildings, and houses.

The capitalist class has, therefore, been remarkably successful in maintaining significantly superior economic life chances to those of the rest of the population. Nevertheless, it is important to note that economic development and welfare policy in the twentieth century have not resulted in an unambiguous *maximization* of the advantages accruing to the capitalist class. This class has, in all probability, seen a real decline in the level of its income and wealth relative to other classes. Indeed, this redistribution may well be seen as a necessary 'concession' to other classes whose electoral and other support is necessary if the capitalist class is to maintain its general economic dominance. It may be suggested that the substantial economic redistribution that has taken place was necessary to sustain a relatively unified power bloc under the dominance of the capitalist business class.

There remain a number of extremely wealthy families within the core of the capitalist business class, and table 4.3 sets out an estimate of the wealth enjoyed by Britain's 20 wealthiest families. Each member of the top 0.1 per cent of wealth holders, it will be recalled, held at least £740,000, but the survey on which table 4.3 is based has estimated that in 1990 there were 200 families with more than £50 million each. Their aggregate wealth amounts to just under 10 per cent of the total gross domestic product. At the top of the league of wealth were the private assets of the Royal family, and the 'top 20' includes a mixture of urban and rural rentier landowners and entrepreneurial capitalists. The research concentrated on rela-

Table 4.3 *Britain's rich (1990)*

Family	Estimated wealth (£m.)	Main source of wealth
1 The Royal family	6,700	land and urban property
2 Grosvenor [Duke of Westminster]	4,200	land and urban property
3 Rausing	2,040	food packaging
4 Sainsbury	1,777	food retailing
5 Weston	1,674	food prodn. and retailing
6 Moores	1,670	football pools, retailing
7 Vestey	1,420	food production
8 Getty	1,350	oil
9 Maxwell	1,100	publishing
10 Feeney	1,020	retailing
11 Hinduja	1,000	trading
12 Livanos	930	shipping
13 Goldsmith	750	retailing and finance
14 Swire	692	shipping and aviation
15 Ronson	548	urban property, petrol distribution
16 Barclay*	500	hotels and urban property
17 Branson	488	music and aviation
18 Cadogan [Earl Cadogan]	450	land and urban property
19 Jerwood	400	trading
20 Portman [Viscount Portman]	400	land and urban property
21 Thompson	400	food processing, property

* Not the family associated with Barclays Bank.
Source: P. Beresford. 'Britain's Rich: The Top 200', *Sunday Times Magazine*, 8 April 1990. This table shows the five largest companies in each sector that were subject to each type of control.

tively visible sources of wealth and was unable to penetrate very far into the anonymity of most shareholdings and bank accounts. For this reason, rentiers, whose assets are concentrated in such anonymous investment portfolios, are under-represented. It is likely, however, that the research correctly identified land and entrepreneurial capital as the major sources of really large fortunes in the 1980s. The wealthiest landowners are the long-established landowning families of Cadogan, Grosvenor, and Portman, most of whom own substantial urban estates as well as their country acres.

The list of the top 20 includes a number of well-known entrepreneurial families who have made their wealth in such areas as retailing, food production, and commerce, and there are signs of an increasing internationalization of wealth at these levels. Not only do many of the entrepreneurial capitalists have substantial interests overseas – this is especially the case for Goldsmith, Weston, Swire, and Vestey – but a number of overseas entrepreneurial capitalists have chosen to settle in Britain: the Rausings from Sweden, Getty and Feeney from the United States, Hinduja from India, and Livanos from Greece. Economic conditions which favour the growth of 'self-made', entrepreneurial fortunes also favour the growth of inherited fortunes and, despite the prominence of entrepreneurial capital, the top 200 is dominated by old, inherited wealth. One hundred and four of the top 200 wealthy families owe the bulk of their present wealth to inheritance. Inherited wealth is also far less risky as a basis for a family fortune. The holdings of those who depend upon a fast growing enterprise for their wealth, for example, are heavily dependent upon the ups and downs of the stock exchange. The personal fortune of Alan Sugar, founder of the Amstrad electronics company, for example, fell from £432m at the beginning of 1989 to £118m in 1990 because of the trouble experienced by his company during the year. At the height of these difficulties, Sugar's fortune declined at the rate of £1m each week. Very few of the family fortunes in the top 200 were the immediate result of inheritance or enterprise by their female members. Apart from the exceptional case of the Royal family, this was true of only four families: those of Anita Roddick, Lady Anne Cavendish-Bentinck, Lady Glover, and Charlotte Morrison. While Anita Roddick's fortune was earned from her Body Shop business, the remaining three female fortunes were based on the inheritance of land.[24]

There are many families in the league of the very rich who appear to be new entrepreneurs with self-made, first-generation fortunes. Research by Harbury and Hitchens, however, has shown that most of these people were 'self-made' in only a very limited sense. The self-made entrepreneurs who rose to these heights did not start empty-handed, but generally had some 'seed corn' of inherited wealth. Inheriting from their own parents in the entrepreneurial middle class or marrying a woman who had inherited wealth from her parents was the way in which many men secured the funds to invest in the ventures which subsequently made their fortunes.[25] This channel of mobility into the capitalist class, therefore, was from the entrepreneurial middle class to entrepreneurial capitalist locations, and their children may be expected to form the rentiers of the future. Indeed, many entrepreneurial capitalists sold their businesses, or a substantial part of them, at the height of their success and so converted themselves to a rentier orientation.

Although property, and the wealth which it generates, is the primary base of capitalist class privileges, it is clear from figure 4.1 that this need not, in every case, be personal property. Those who hold directorships in large enterprises occupy capitalist locations, and if the income from their employment is substantial they may be able to sustain a relatively secure foothold within the capitalist class. Where they or other members of their household are property holders, this position may be more secure. But where their privileges depend exclusively on a high earned income, secure class privileges may be gained only if this income is used to accumulate substantial wealth. I have already shown, however, that the possibilities for accumulating wealth in this way are very limited unless there is already some seed-corn wealth, and the chances of a full-time director being able to convert a high income, received at a relatively late stage in their career, into substantial wealth is very small indeed. For this reason, the dividing line between the capitalist class and the service class is difficult to draw with any precision.

There are, nevertheless, a number of extremely well-paid directors whose position within the capitalist class seems secure. Table 4.4 shows Britain's highest paid directors. Some of these are entrepreneurial capitalists who are able to command high salaries by virtue of their direct control of particular companies, but many are executive capitalists and finance capitalists without such a base in inherited wealth. Even these people, however, invariably hold substantial block of shares in their companies – often acquired through share option schemes – and they will earn additional income from the dividends received on these shares. Lord Hanson, 'Tiny' Rowland, and Cyril Stein are all controllers or the representatives of controlling families in major enterprises. Sir Peter Walters and Sir

Table 4.4 *Britain's highest-paid directors (1990)*

	Company	Annual Salary (£)
Lord Hanson	Hanson Trust	1,530,000
Tiny Rowland	Lonrho	1,310,000
Dick Giordano	BOC	937,000
Sir Ralph Halpern	Burton Group	899,000
Sir Kit McMahon	Midland Bank	725,844
Sir Peter Walters	BP	708,722
Geoff Mulcahy	Kingfisher	701,000
Cyril Stein	Ladbroke	603,000
Sir Paul Girolami	Glaxo	598,081
Sir Denys Henderson	ICI	514,000
Allen Sheppard	Grand Metropolitan	506,438

Source: *The Guardian*, 3 May 1990, p. 9.

Denys Henderson, on the other hand, are executive capitalists at the head of two of Britain's largest enterprises. The ability of these people to determine their own level of rewards is clear from the fact that their earnings rose five times faster than the rate of inflation and almost three times faster than the general rise in wage levels. Average rises for the top-paid directors over the period 1985 to 1989 were 120 per cent, and Lord King, the Chairman of British Airways, was awarded an annual rise of 116 per cent in 1989. Those who sit as part-time, non-executive directors of other companies, playing the role of finance capitalist, accumulate additional income from their directors' fees – ranging from a typical £5,000 to such top levels as £100,000. Lord Stevens, for example, is chairman of nine companies and a director of many others. His Chairman's fees for two of these companies were in the region of £250,000 each, and another chairmanship earned him £178,000. The majority of top directors also participate in subsidized share purchase schemes which boost their wealth and give them a further dividend income.

The bases of the income and wealth of the capitalist class are the large business units from which they benefit, both directly and indirectly. The significance of personal controlling holdings has, of course, declined over the course of the century, and personal wealth is now very dependent on the benefits which accrue from the structure of impersonal capital created by the growth of institutional ownership. The amalgamation of family enterprises into large national concerns, which took place around the turn of the century and in the years leading up to the First World War was an important factor in boosting the number of rentier capitalists with interests in the corporate system as a whole.[26] This shift in ownership was, however, a prelude to the expansion of institutional ownership which characterized the inter-war years and which became especially marked after the Second World War. Investment companies had long been involved in the ownership of company shares, but during the 1930s insurance companies and the new unit trusts became active investors on the stock exchange, and pensions funds became especially important from the 1960s. In 1957, two thirds of the capital in large British enterprises was owned by families and individuals, and financial institutions held one fifth. By 1981, these proportions had been almost reversed: families and individuals held 28 per cent and institutions held 58 per cent. In percentage terms, entrepreneurial and rentier holdings declined as significant elements in the capital of many of the largest enterprises, and the various forms of family control began to give way to control through a constellation of interests. Rentier families now invest alongside the big institutions and through the institutions themselves. The merchant banks and investment branches of the large clearing banks, for example, manage the investment portfolios of many wealthy families, and the involvement of these families on their boards is one way of ensuring that they are managed in accordance with their interests.

The land sales which followed the First World War led, in one estimate, to one quarter of England changing hands between 1918 and 1922.[27] Absentee landowners sold land to their tenants and to others interested in farming the land. The percentage of farmland that was 'owner-occupied' rose from about 10 per cent in 1914 to 36 per cent in 1927. By the 1970s this figure had risen to more than 60 per cent. Although this reflects a real growth in the number of owner-farmers, at the expense of the tenant farmers, it also reflects an increasing tendency for landowners to consolidate their holdings and take them 'in hand' to farm the land for themselves. The old landowning families have not completely disappeared: they have been transformed. The high percentage of owner-occupied land is an outcome of the transformation of both the 'traditional' landed rentier and the old tenant farmer into new-style entrepreneurial agrarian capitalists.

There has, however, been a further change in the pattern of land ownership. Just as personal share ownership in industry and finance has been squeezed by institutional share ownership, so the ownership of farm land has come into the hands of these same institutions.

Plate 4.1 Capitalist Agriculture. A combine harvester in East Anglia: the mechanization of large-scale agriculture. (Reproduced by kind permission of Dr John B. Free, Heritage and Natural History Photography.)

Institutional ownership is, in one sense, nothing new. 'Institutions' such as the Church of England and the colleges of Oxford and Cambridge, have long been major landowners, but these are not financial 'institutions'. The traditional landowning 'institutions' are simply corporate bodies, as distinct from individual and family owners. The modern 'institutions' are the financial intermediaries and investors of the City of London – the banks, insurance companies, and pensions funds. City institutions have had a great impact on agricultural land since the 1960s, just as they have had on urban land and on industry. Nevertheless, the City institutions still own less than 1 per cent of the total agricultural land in Britain; albeit land of the highest agricultural quality.

Table 4.5 shows the relative significance of the various forms of landownership today. Despite the growth of institutional land-ownership, over a half of the land area remains in the ownership of families and family trusts. Some of the land recorded as owned by companies other than the financial institutions is owned by industrial undertakings as part of their business operations, but much of this, too, is family-owned land which is registered in the names of private family companies.

Plate 4.2 The City of London: skyline of city. (Skyscan Balloon Photography Copyright.)

How can the anatomy of the capitalist class be summarized? It is a class which is increasingly dependent on the system of impersonal capital which has resulted from the growth of institutional property holdings. The business enterprises subject to institutional control, to control through a constellation of interests, buttress the continued wealth of the families with financial interests in the corporate sector and in land, and the support of the institutions is fundamental for the incomes of those dependent on careers in the large corporate bureaucracies. The rentiers with system-wide interests in the modern capitalist economy are those whose interests are most closely tied to the sphere of impersonal capital: their own financial holdings are invested in and managed by the financial institutions, and they constitute a large pool of families from whom the finance capitalists who sit on the boards of the institutions are recruited. Alongside the entrepreneurial capitalists, 'passive' rentiers, and executive capitalists is the 'inner circle' of finance capitalists with directorships in two or more very large enterprises in the system of impersonal

Table 4.5 *Post-war landownership*

Landowners	% of land held
State (central and local)	19
Royal family & Crown Estate	1
Church of England, charities, Oxbridge colleges	
Families and trusts	3
Financial institutions	54
Other companies	1
	5

Source: D. Massey and A. Catalano, *Capital and Land*, Edward Arnold (London, 1978), table 3–6, p. 59. The figures in the table do not add up to 100% because estimates were made on differing bases. The figures are intended to give only an indication of the relative significance of each group. Data relate to various dates in the 1960s and 1970s.

capital. Occupants of all these capitalist locations are able to secure advantaged opportunities and life chances for their families and to live a life of privilege.

Class Reproduction and Capital Reproduction

The part played by entrepreneurial capital in the British economy has declined since the end of the nineteenth century. For the later Fabian writers and the theorists of the 'managerial revolution', this was linked to the belief that the capitalist class was disappearing. The shrinking of the sphere of personal possession, it was held, would see the replacement of capitalist entrepreneurs by non-capitalist salaried managers. I have tried to show that entrepreneurial capitalists have not completely disappeared – far from it – and that rentier capitalists have become an increasingly important force alongside the growth of impersonal institutional capital. But if the capitalist class has not disappeared, it is clear that the structure of the class and the mechanisms through which it is reproduced have altered.

The reality glimpsed by managerialist writers is, in fact, a partial dissociation of the mechanisms of *class reproduction* from those of *capital reproduction*. Executive and finance capitalist locations are central to the reproduction of capital within the sphere of impersonal possession and those who occupy these locations, together with those in service-class locations, are the 'managers' of institutional capital. But this involvement in the reproduction of capital does not necessarily mean that they simultaneously reproduce a privileged and self-perpetuating capitalist class.

It is possible, in principle, for there to be free and open access to these capitalist and service locations, with all positions held by salaried bureaucrats who subside into middle class obscurity on completion of their business careers. In fact, I have shown, this is not the case. Executive capitalist and, especially, finance capitalist locations are occupied by those from an entrepreneurial or rentier background. Although the personal wealth and privileges of these people and their families depend upon the operations of the impersonal institutions and large enterprises in which many of them hold directorships, the institutions and large enterprises do not, themselves, depend on their presence on their boards. Rentier capitalists depend upon the system of impersonal possession, but the reproduction of the system of impersonal possession does not necessarily result in the reproduction of the rentiers themselves. The rentier capitalists who monopolize executive and finance capitalist locations depend upon other mechanisms for the reproduction of their rentier locations and class privileges.[28] An important avenue for enquiry is how this class reproduction is to be explained.

The reproduction of a capitalist class involves the reproduction of a structure of intermarried households with similar life chances. The class reproduction of entrepreneurial capitalists in Britain today poses few problems for class theory, as the mechanisms involved are analogous to those involved in the reproduction of the nineteenth-century entrepreneurs. Their class reproduction is a direct consequence of their personal ownership and control of capital. Although the system of personal property holding has become more complex in its structure, reliance on direct personal shareholdings for majority or minority control is nothing new. But the class reproduction of rentier capitalists has been inadequately theorized. The rentiers of the twentieth century differ from the landed rentiers of earlier centuries in the sheer spread of their propertied interests. They depend upon diversified sources of wealth holding, and their assets are system-wide in their scope and extent. Their property consists predominantly of institutional assets – bank deposits, shares managed by trust companies, etc., – and so their wealth and income depend upon the operation of the system of impersonal possession. To the extent that rentiers are able to participate in corporate rule, as executive and finance capitalists, they have a direct supervisory position in the affairs of the system on which their privileges depend.

By taking on these positions, they are able to ensure that the system continues to advantage them through its operations. Their recruitment to these locations is not a simple matter of merit and talent, but reflects the advantages accorded by the possession of a particular kind of social background. This background of property and privilege allows the link between capital and class reproduction to be sustained. Rentiers are able to monopolize access to these locations through the informal networks of social connections which bind the wealthy together. These social networks, rooted in family and schooling, are important elements in class reproduction. They are the topic of the following chapter.

5 Is there still an Upper Circle?

In the previous chapter I looked at the development of a unified capitalist business class from the separate nineteenth-century capitalist classes of land, commerce, and industry. In Chapter 3 I showed that, in the early stages of its history, the capitalist business class was structured around a dominant status group, a single upper circle of status superiors who also comprised the basis of a political establishment. The aim of this chapter is to outline the nature of the nineteenth-century upper circle a little more fully and to assess whether there is still an upper circle in Britain today.

Much of this chapter will be concerned with documenting the cultural dimension of status – the language of status differentiation and the life styles with which this is associated. But status factors are also important as elements in class reproduction, especially in circumstances where the direct personal inheritance of economic locations does not take place. Status differentiation through language, socialization, and interaction establishes informal social networks of kinship, friendship, and acquaintance which can become important supplements to economic inheritance. These social networks, grounded in traditionally sanctioned status, are central elements in class reproduction.

The 'Traditional' Status System

The landed class of the old society had defined itself as a dominant status group of 'gentlemen', an upper circle of status superiors which was sharply divided from the commonalty of all grades. On the basis of the life chances they derived from their economic locations as owners of agrarian capital, the landed gentlemen and their families pursued a privileged way of life from which members of other classes were excluded. Their contact with those outside their own class were few and far between. With their tenants, lawyers, and bankers they were involved in a variety of necessary but limited business transactions; and their contacts with the mass of servants and retainers who supported their life style were cursory in the extreme. When a landed gentleman spoke of 'Society', he had in mind the society of gentlemen and their families: those in the common herd simply did not 'count'; they were not regarded as a part of Society.

This view became even more firmly entrenched during the nineteenth century. The increasing number of wealthy industrialists and financiers posed a stronger threat to the continued dominance of the landed gentlemen in the status hierarchy. As they came to redefine themselves as an 'aristocracy' or an 'upper class', so they also attempted to re-affirm their distinctiveness from the mere middle classes. Forced to recognize the economic advantages and political power of 'new wealth', the aristocracy attempted to ensure some continued recognition of their status superiority. The word 'Society', generally with a capital 'S', was extended to describe those who mattered in terms of the established status values. Those who mattered were the landed aristocracy and the families of those wealthy industrial and commercial capitalists who accepted the continuing dominance of the old landowners. As landowners accepted a degree of economic and political accommodation with the new capitalist forces, they came to regard the families of new wealth as more acceptable status equals, so long as they did not challenge the *values* of the landowners. The framework of 'elitism' was adapted to the new circumstances of the nineteenth century. From the standpoint of its members, Society was the upper circle of the status hierarchy. It was the 'polite society' of 'the best'. From the standpoint of those in the lower circles, however, it was the 'high society' of the privileged few.

'Society' was a cohesive status group at the core of the capitalist class, a status group which emphasized a particular cultural outlook, a life style, and a code of practice, and so reinforced the social closure which was exercised by the capitalist class as a whole. The word 'Society' also came to describe the complex of institutions and practices which made up the life style of the upper circle of the wealthy. These institutions and practices defined the boundaries and the distinctiveness of the established social groups, and allowed them to exercise some control over the admittance of outsiders.

Although newcomers might enter capitalist locations and secure a place for themselves and their families in the foothills of the capitalist class, they could still be denied entry to its upper circle. The unacceptable new rich were socially excluded by the claims to 'traditional' status which were made by those with 'old money' and which were embodied in the institutions and practices of Society. Conversely, those who were granted entry to Society, once their wealth had 'matured' or they had otherwise earned their acceptance, could be accorded recognition as full members of the upper circle.[1]

The life style of the Society families of the eighteenth century had been very much a county affair, centred around Quarter Sessions and estate business. London was the parliamentary and official centre to which county business was orientated and around which a number of social activities took place during the parliamentary season from February to August. Some other towns played a similar, though lesser role in social affairs for their counties, becoming important foci for landed-class activities during the autumn and winter months. Such places as Bath, Harrogate, and Scarborough did, however, play an important regional and national role in leisure activities.

It was this round of activities which, during the course of the nineteenth century, underwent a transformation and resulted in the establishment of polite or high society. As more of the new rich were granted entry to the upper circle, the boundaries of Society broadened in the same direction as the boundaries of the dominant class itself. As the three capitalist classes of land, commerce, and industry moved towards full merger as a unified business class, so its dominant status group formed around the institutions and practices of Society. High society became more national in scope, with London playing an even greater role than formerly. London Society developed an ascendant position over provincial Society.

At the heart of this system was the Royal family and the Court, which played a key role in the regulation of Society and in articulating it with the state apparatus. The Royal family were, of course, among the country's principal landowners, and it was through the Royal Court that the official business of the state had, during the eighteenth century, been integrated with county affairs and with the informal social activities of the landed class. Most executive functions of government became separated from the Royal Court, but it remained, throughout the nineteenth century, an integral part of the state machinery. And while its political role declined, its role at the head of Society became increasingly important.

Membership of Society depended upon acceptance by those whose membership was established and unquestioned. Those who aspired to membership required the sponsorship of others, already established, who would introduce them to the kind of people and activities that would improve their own chances of acceptance. Formal rituals of introduction and recognition permeated Society, and an introduction to the sovereign was the ultimate sign of acceptance. Presentation at Court was the official mark of recognition and acceptability.

With the growth in the size of Society, presentations at Court became much more numerous and, therefore, more formalized. Rich financiers and industrialists were less likely to be known personally by members of the Royal family or the established landowners, and Court presentations involved complex chains of sponsorship. Equally, there could be no guarantee that those already 'in' Society would know that a particular individual had been successfully presented and was, therefore, acceptable as a status equal within the upper circle. If newcomers to Society were to achieve their due recognition, signs or indicators of acceptability were required. Reflecting this greater diversity and the need for objective arbiters of status was a rash of directories and handbooks which listed not only peers, baronets, and knights, but also the untitled families of the 'gentry'. Burke's *Landed Gentry*, for example, began publication in 1833, and it rapidly became a semi-official register of acceptability in Society.[2] Certificates of Presentation were issued by the Royal Court from 1854, and these gave their holders an indisputable passport to the other institutions of Society.

The Court was also responsible, together with the Prime Minister, for the awarding of titles and honours. Though increasingly determined by the government rather than by the sovereign, titular and other honours were nominally awarded in the name of the Crown and were received from the monarch in person. The publication of tables of precedence, indicating who should precede whom in official functions and social gatherings, ensured that everyone 'knew their place' in the complex hierarchy of the upper circle. The king or queen, as the 'Fount of Honour', stood at the head of the system of honours and precedence, and so accorded official accreditation to the judgments of Society and linked its activities with the operations of the state and the established church. As Davidoff remarks: 'State Balls at Buckingham Palace, Royal entertainments and Royal attendance at certain functions gave a stamp of authority to the whole fabric of Society'.[3]

Central to Society was its social code, its prescriptions and prohibitions concerning what was 'done' and what was 'not done'. An extensive body of norms regulated the minutiae of day-to-day interactions from greetings and meetings to times of eating. The code structured the kinship-related events of birth, death, and, above all, marriage, and it sanctioned particular patterns of gender and sexuality (see box 5.1). Though separate from the operations of the world of work itself, the social code involved firm ideas about the kind and amount of work that was appropriate for a gentleman. The application of this social code in a society structured around the inherited social round of the landed class led to the institutionalization of a rigid social calendar, a sequence of social events interwoven with the demands of public life and the requirements of leisure.[4] The male-dominated worlds of politics and sport defined a central schedule of events for the social calendar, and this was the framework around which a myriad of informal events arose. It was also, and most importantly, the basis of the London 'Season', the parties, balls, and other events through which women sought to regulate the marriages of their daughters and sons.

The London Season got into full swing in May and lasted until the end of July (See box 5.2). During this time, all members of Society would live in or close to London in order to participate in the major events of the social calendar and to be able to enter into the daily and weekly round of social activities. The main sports – horse racing, rowing, tennis, polo, and cricket – each involved a number of key events at which all had to be 'seen', and these and other events provided the occasions for informal parties and more formal dinners. The Season ended with a mass migration to Cowes for the yachting, before the gentlemen and their families returned to their country homes for the autumn round of shooting, hunting,[5] and 'county' activities. Winter brought a slowdown in Society activities until the improvement in the weather in the early spring heralded the beginning of the move back to London for the new Season.

The emergence of Society, the social code, and the social calendar must be seen in relation to an alteration in patterns of leisure and social closure among the privileged. In the old society, the leisure pursuits of the landed gentlemen were, of course, sharply distinguished from those of the lower orders – indeed, precious few of the latter had any real opportunity for 'leisure' in any case. Even where the landed gentlemen participated in public leisure events, the factor of cost served to ensure that they had little contact with their inferiors. Where public entertainments were open to all who could afford them, the landed gentlemen could be sure that it was,

Box 5.1 *Manners and rules of good society*

Meetings and Introductions

Calls made in the morning – that is before one o'clock – would not come under denomination of 'morning calls', as they can only be made by intimate friends and not by acquaintances, and are not, therefore, amenable to the rules of etiquette which govern the afternoon calls, which calls are regulated in a great measure – as to the hour of calling – by the exact degree of intimacy existing between the person who calls and the person called upon. From three to four o'clock is the ceremonious hour for calling; from four to five o'clock is the semi-ceremonious hour; and from five to six o'clock is the wholly friendly hour and without ceremony hour.

As regards the routine of card-leaving when driving, a lady should desire her man-servant to inquire if the mistress of the house at which she is calling is 'at home'. If 'not at home' she should hand him *three* cards: *one* of her own, and *two* of her husband's; but if her husband's name is printed on her card, *one* of his cards only would be required; her card is left for the mistress of the house, and her husband's cards for both master and mistress.

It is the rule for a gentleman to ask a mutual friend, or an acquaintance, for an introduction to a lady, and it is the received rule to do so when a gentleman desires to be introduced to any lady in particular; but gentlemen do not ask to be introduced to each other, unless some special reason exists for so doing.

The usual hours for walking, both in the metropolis and at watering-places or seaside towns, are from twelve to two o'clock; but persons not possessing carriages would of course walk in the afternoon also, the hours for afternoon walking ranging from three o'clock to half past four in the winter, and from three o'clock to six o'clock in the summer.

At Dinner

The host and hostess should come forward and shake hands with each guest on arrival. The ladies should at once seat themselves, but gentlemen either stand about the room and talk to each other, or sit down after a wait of some minutes.

On dinner being announced, the host should give his right arm to the lady of highest rank present, and, with her, lead the way to the dining room, followed by the lady second in rank, with a gentleman second in rank and so on. The gentleman of highest rank present should follow last with the hostess.

Death and Mourning

For a parent the period of mourning is twelve months, six months black with crape, four months black without crape, two months half mourning.

Linen collars and cuffs should not be worn during the crape period, but crape lisse only. Neither should jewellery be worn during the crape period, nor until the first two months of black have expired.

The regulation period for a widow's mourning is two years . . . A widow is not expected to enter into society under twelve months, and during that time she should neither accept invitations nor issue them. Her visiting should be confined to her relations and intimate friends. After twelve months she should commence gradually to enter into society, but balls and dances should be avoided during the period that crape is worn.

Source: Manners and Rules of Good Society, by a Member of the Aristocracy, 17th edn (Frederick Warne, London, 1891), pp. 30, 18, 8, 181, 99, 101, 223, 226.

in fact, only the socially acceptable who were able to afford them. In the altered circumstances of the nineteenth century, with an expansion in the numbers of the wealthy, this was no longer the case. Among the upper circle there occurred, around the middle of the century, what might be called a 'privatization' of sociability. In order to exclude those who were unacceptable, some barrier other than price had to be erected. Activities that were formerly public

---

Box 5.2 *The social calendar*

Beginning of the London Season

May	The first garden parties, Court presentations, and balls.
	Queen Charlotte's Ball
	Royal Academy Summer Exhibition
	Covent Garden opera season opens
	Royal Military Tournament
	Royal Horticultural Society Show [Chelsea Flower Show]
June	The Derby [Epsom]
	Fourth of June [Eton speech day and cricket]
	Ascot racing week [Gold Cup]
	Trooping the Colour and Birthday Honours List
July	Wimbledon fortnight
	Polo at Hurlingham
	Oxford and Cambridge cricket match
	Eton and Harrow cricket match
	Henley Regatta
	Goodwood racing

Close of the London Season

August	Cowes week
	Grouse shooting begins
	Stag hunting begins
September	Partridge shooting begins
	Cubbing begins
October	Pheasant shooting begins
November	Fox hunting begins
	First county balls
	State Opening of Parliament
January	New Year Honours List
March	Cheltenham National Hunt racing [Gold Cup]
	Grand National [Aintree]
April	Oxford and Cambridge boat race

The dates of some of the above events varied from year to year, so the months shown are general indications only.

– open to all – became private, activities to which only those of recognized social standing were admitted. In this way, firm controls over participation could be asserted.

Davidoff has linked this process of privatization to a sharpening of the division between the public spheres of business and politics and the private sphere of the household.[6] This separation developed first in wealthy manufacturing families and, from the first third of the nineteenth century, it spread to virtually all wealthy families. The confinement of women, to a greater extent than before, to the private world of house and family became a fundamental norm of Society. The power that women exercised – and for many women of the upper circle this was considerable – was exercised in and through their role within the family household. They managed the formal and ritualized round of visits and introductions through which recognition and acceptance were negotiated and access to the private world of the privileged was granted. Women at home were able to be 'At Home' to callers who came in person or left their visiting cards. In addition to their role in the provision of dinners, house parties, and other entertainments for friends and acquaintances, women were able to play a major role in determining access to the other privatized activities of Society. Important balls and functions ceased to be subscription or ticket affairs and came under the tight control of private hostesses. The remaining large public functions were often preceded by smaller and more exclusive private dinners and parties.

The privatization of sociability among the privileged was associated also with greater residential segregation in the expanding towns. Although the classes continued to live cheek-by-jowl in many of the older areas of London, there was a tendency for the new West End of Mayfair and Belgravia to become the fashionable and exclusive territory of the upper circle and their servants. Proximity to parliament and the Court, and to Hyde Park and Kensington Park, made the West End the natural home of the privileged. Provincial towns and cities developed their local equivalents of the West End, where the leaders of local Society congregated at a safe distance from the middle and working classes.

The private sphere of family and household, the dominant sphere of action for women, was tied to the institutions of Society through its involvement in the arrangement and control of marriages. A good marriage was essential for the survival of a wealthy family and its property, but it was also important for the autonomy of women themselves. A woman's status in Society depended on that of her husband or father. As an unmarried woman remained subordinate to her parents, marriage, for all that it subordinated women to their husbands, was of extreme importance to them.

The Society balls and dances were places where young women could be introduced to eligible young men under controlled and supervised conditions. Eligibility for invitations to important dances was associated with 'coming out' into Society. This was the point at which a young woman officially entered Society. Ideally this took place at a Court presentation, but for many a local function would launch the woman into the first 'Season' of her adulthood. Within two, or at most three Seasons a woman was expected to have found a suitable marriage partner, though the hostesses who controlled the functions of the Season were equally concerned that their sons should make appropriate marriages.

Motherhood was, among the wealthy, a sign of success in the family strategy – more obviously so if the child was a boy. Ladies were not, however, expected to be involved in the upbringing of their children. The ideal of domesticity saw them as the managers of the domestic sphere, delegating the actual domestic work to others. Just as cleaning, cooking, and the whole daily routine of household tasks were delegated to domestic servants, so the socialization of children was delegated to nannies and governesses.

The public spheres of business and politics, dominated by men, were integrally linked with a cluster of institutions through which men were prepared for entry to the public world and through which their public activities continued to be sustained. These institutions were the 'public' schools and universities and the 'private' gentlemen's clubs. The former provided a degree of formal education and 'character building' but, above all, established the social connections which could ensure access to a satisfactory public position. The private clubs provided a venue at which the connections which had been made at school and at university could be renewed, reinforced, and elaborated throughout a person's adult life. It was through these mechanisms that family strategy was linked with occupational placement.

For the eldest sons of wealthy families, inheritance of the family estate or the family firm was a direct and straightforward way of ensuring the perpetuation of privileges. Younger sons, however, had always had to rely on the patronage and sponsorship of those who could help them to obtain a suitable position. The networks of connection which linked the leading families were, therefore, important mechanisms of social plaement. With the vast expansion of the state apparatus in the nineteenth century, the growing scale and complexity of economic enterprise, the shift from personal to impersonal ownership and the associated expansion in the number of wealthy families, the direct inheritance of positions became far less important, even for the eldest sons. But these changes also made it impossible to rely upon the old practices of purely personal

Plate 5.1 Oxford's Dreaming Spires. (Reproduced by kind permission of Mr S. Maybury.)

patronage. The reformed public schools and the Oxford and Cambridge colleges provided an excellent substitute for the patronage system. The 'old boy network' which was built through the institutions of school, university, and club was the basis through which recruitment in business and politics could be organized and through which career mobility could be structured. Rooted as it was in networks of kinship and intermarriage, the old boy network mediated the private world of family and kinship with the public world of business and politics.

By the end of the nineteenth century, high society had expanded considerably, reflecting the growth and gradual merger of the capitalist classes of land, commerce and industry. A contemporary estimate put its size at around 4 000 families – about 0.05 per cent of the population. This upper circle of Society families stood at the top of the status hierarchy and gave a veneer of 'tradition' to the power and resources of the capitalist class. It accorded the whole class structure a degree of legitimacy and masked the divisions and contradictions which beset the classes of Victorian and Edwardian Britain.

The high society of the public world and the London salons,

restaurants, and ballrooms was articulated with similar but less powerful and less established upper circles in provincial cities and larger towns across the country. In the absence of many of the very wealthy, who preferred to spend the Season in London, smaller landowners, merchants, manufacturers, and farmers were there able to play a leading role and to involve aspiring members of the professional and entrepreneurial middle classes in a subordinate capacity in their social activities. In this way, the electoral support which the power bloc required could be reinforced through day-to-day contacts.

But high society and its provincial outliers did not form a perfectly consensual and unified status order. Alongside the divisions between the cosmopolitans and the provincials, and between one country and another, were divisions into separate social circles centred around particular specialist activities and interests: the racing and the gambling 'sets' and the literary and 'intellectual' cliques, for example, were especially important and formed distinct social circles within the capitalist class. The social circles of the wealthy Quaker, Catholic, and Jewish families, and certain other religious groups, also tended to follow their own distinct circuits of activities and to construct their own networks of mutual support. The top of the national status hierarchy, therefore, comprised a cluster of intersecting social circles centred around the aristocratic, 'upper class' high society.

Many of the new rich, however, found no place for themselves within this system. They found themselves excluded from Society activities by both the metropolitan and the provincial upper circles. In addition, many of the new rich were indifferent to or had rejected the status claims of the upper circles. Nevertheless, through links of kinship and schooling as well as through their business and political activities, many of these families were gradually able, if they wished, to achieve a degree of acceptance by the established members of the upper circles. On this basis a sufficient degree of consensus and cohesion existed among the leading capitalist families for them to be able to sustain the solidarity of a power bloc.

The status hierarchy headed by the upper circle, like many systems of status, was projected as a 'traditional' status order. Despite very obvious signs of change and social transformation, the basic features of society were seen as fundamentally unchanging. Land, property, and the values associated with them were seen as the 'normal' and 'natural' bases of privilege and power. This was the way, it was claimed, that things had always been. But as the emergent capitalist business class was a novel feature of the late nineteenth century, these self-justifications cannot be taken at face value. The framework of 'traditional' values which legitimated capitalist powers and privileges was, in fact, the creation of that very class. This framework of legitimation drew heavily on the values and ideas of the old landed aristocracy, but these were welded into a coherent meaning system which was able to justify the dominance of property in all its forms. From the 1870s can be recognized the creation of a series of imperial 'traditions', a process that was of crucial importance in restructuring the monarchy and adjusting it to a continuing role as legitimator of Britain's archaic social structure.[7] Despite the impact of democratization, industrialization, and urbanization, the British social order was wedded to the archaic ideas of the old landed class.

One reason why the values of the landowners held a central position in the framework of legitimation was that the idea of 'England' as an area of land could easily be equated with the idea of 'England' as a cultural and political entity. What more natural than that those who owned the physical reality of the English countryside should determine the principles which should govern English society? The immovability and permanence of land was equated with the stability of society. And in an imperial society, the distinction between 'England' and 'Britain' was easily glossed. The acceptance of this kind of view by industrialists – or, at least, their failure to formulate a coherent challenge to its continuing hegemony – meant that there was a continuing impetus towards the purchase of land, albeit on a small scale, by the newly rich. Buying land was a token of acceptance of the established order and a claim to a voice in public affairs. The predominance of landowners and their values was further reinforced by their success in retaining the criterion of 'pedigree' in association with property ownership. What was important was a personal link with the land, and so those who could trace this link back over the generations were able to emphasize their own superior rights to social and political power.

The British capitalist class was not simply a plutocracy of wealth. The claims of 'mere' money were evaluated against the measuring sticks of land and pedigree. For this reason, those without land sought the surrogate status symbols of peerages, baronetcies, knighthoods, and similar 'honours'. For a wealthy manufacturer, a title without an estate or a long pedigree was almost as good as the real thing, especially if a respectable genealogy could be constructed or a small plot of land could be bought. In this way they could gain a recognized position in the great hierarchy of 'traditional' status presided over by the monarchy.

'Tradition', Social Networks and Class Reproduction

How much of this 'traditional' status system persisted into the twentieth century? Strains and tensions within the life style of the upper circle were already apparent by the end of the nineteenth century. Agricultural depression and the need for landowners to secure ever greater cash injections for their estates put the landed aristocracy under great financial pressure. More attention had to be given to the efficient business management of their estates and to finding ways of improving their financial prospects. Correspondingly less time and fewer resources could be given over to leisured participation in Society activities. At the same time, parliamentary and local government reforms lessened their political dominance and introduced a separation of Society activities from the official world of the state. High society became less exclusive, and there was an increasing willingness to accept 'new' wealth on equal terms with 'old' wealth. Intermarriage between landowning, commercial, and industrial families became more frequent, and a unified capitalist class was formed. Industrial and commercial wealth became crucial for the financial survival of many landowners, and the new rich of industry and commerce were eager purchasers for that land which had to be sold. Landed aristocrats diversified their wealth to a far greater extent than ever before, and took more active roles on the boards of joint stock companies.

This accommodation with industrial and commercial wealth was reflected in the part played by the Prince of Wales (later Edward VII) in securing the acceptance of the plutocrats at Court and in Society activities. Edwardian Society was, in consequence, more ostentatious, more concerned with pleasure and money, than had been Victorian Society, reflecting both the changed attitudes towards wealth among landowners and the far greater participation of industrial and commercial wealth in public life generally. The Edwardian period also saw the withdrawal, for financial reasons, of many of the lesser landowning families who had previously formed the backbone of county and London Society. Many could no longer afford the expense of the London Season and retreated to country activities. While becoming less exclusive, therefore, high society became a much smaller social circle. The smaller plutocratic upper circle became relatively more detached from the other social circles which made up the status hierarchy of the capitalist class.

The First World War reinforced this transformation of high society. Few wealthy families survived the war without the loss of a young family member, and for many there were problems over inheritance and estate duty. While the inter-war years saw a growth in capitalist involvement in leisure activities and in the 'pursuit of pleasure',[8] this was no longer contained within the framework of high society. No longer was the round of Society activities and the London Season the undisputed pinnacle of the status system. Detached from any official involvement in matters of state, the London Season became a purely private affair. Society and the Season were central to the search for marriage partners for many wealthy families, and many of its members continued to play an important part in politics, but it was no longer central to the mechanisms of state power. Despite its prominence and visibility in the gossip columns of the newspapers, high society had become simply one of a number of equally legitimate and equally privileged patterns of leisure in a complex of intersecting social circles within the capitalist class.

During the inter-war years the grander families who sought to maintain the framework of Society began to come under greater strain. The period saw an increased concern with the impact of declining rents and increased levels of taxation. There were enormous costs involved in maintaining the big London houses which had been the cornerstones of the London Season. The First World War had heralded a period of economic transformation in which greater employment opportunities and higher wages, especially for women, reduced the supply of those who were willing to enter into domestic service. Although wealthy families managed to get by with fewer servants, they found it difficult to sustain even a small town house on the kind of scale that would have been normal before the war. The response of many was to sell their London houses. Mayfair became a district of hotels, embassies, flats and offices. Leisure activities which had formerly been privately pursued in the great houses had to be transferred to more public restaurants and night clubs. This meant that social exclusion had to be more strictly on grounds of cost rather than of acceptability to the established arbiters of status. High society became something of a façade, its reality of privilege and conspicuous consumption being increasingly difficult to project as a 'traditional' feature of British society.

The Second World War and the conditions of the post-war economy put the final seal on large-scale domestic service. War work and the growing peace-time demand for women workers in industry meant that low-wage domestic service was no longer the main employment option available to women. The large country houses also came under pressure from the decline of domestic service and, like their London counterparts, many were transformed into businesses or were sold. One way of maintaining the house was to 'open' it to the public and to use the house and estate as a commercial leisure and entertainment enterprise, as a 'stately home', rather than an agricultural and social one. Those houses which were sold went increasingly to corporate rather than to individual purchasers, and they became corporate headquarters, country hotels, schools, conference halls, and sports centres. Relatively few of the big country houses were able to survive one or other of these fates.

There remains today a residue of the old high society families who, together with some newcomers, pursue some of the same round of activities, with members of the Royal family still playing a central part. But these activities are completely dissociated from official political involvement, presentation of débutantes at Court ended in 1958, and these families no longer hold an undisputed position at the top of the status hierarchy. Their organization is more diffuse and less closed to outsiders – indeed, many of the 'new' rich are among its most active participants. It is this social circle that *Harper's and Queen's* magazine caricatured as the 'Sloane Ranger' set.[9]

For these families the débutante Season remains important, involving about 150 young women every year. Beginning now with the NSPCC Berkeley Dress Show at the beginning of April the Season proceeds through the Rose Ball and the Caledonian Ball, with the Queen Charlotte Ball rounding off the Season in September. Today, 'doing the Season' is important for the networking opportunities that it offers the women. Contacts made during the Season can be drawn on in later years for career openings, as well as providing the basis for meeting potential marriage partners. The cost of the Season is considerable. It has been estimated that, on top of annual school fees of £6,000 or more, the parents of a débutante might have to spend £5,000 on dresses and, if they hold a dance of their own, £40,000 for catering and entertainment.

There is no longer an undisputed upper circle to the status hierarchy. The status circles of the capitalist class are numerous. Instead of a single upper circle there is a complex of intersecting upper circles. The residential territory of these upper circles in London is no longer restricted to Mayfair, but is spread throughout the more westerly districts of London. The wealthiest private households are now centred on Belgravia, Knightsbridge, and Chelsea, with substantial outcrops striking north into Holland Park, St John's Wood, and Regent's Park, and south west into Barnes, Richmond, and Wimbledon. Other areas of central London include dense pockets of wealth, but nowhere outside Belgravia, Knightsbridge and Chelsea are there such concentrations combined with the almost complete exclusion of mere middle-class households. Outside London, all major towns and cities have their wealthy districts, and there are many large houses around villages across the country, but wealth is heavily concentrated in the south and the west. The Home Counties have a greater proportion of wealthy households than any other region, with there being particular concentrations in the westerly districts of Berkshire, Buckinghamshire and Oxfordshire: Ascot, Marlow, and Henley are especially popular areas for wealthy households. Beyond the Home Counties, the counties of Gloucestershire, Wiltshire, Hampshire, and Sussex form the capitalist-class homelands.

There is a high level of interdependence between the wealthy households in south-west London and those in the south-west counties. In some cases there is life cycle mobility: established families live in the country and their independent children take flats in London until they too marry and move out into the country. In other cases, families own both a London house and a country house – both smaller than those of their predecessors of earlier generations – and they commute between the two according to the demands of work and leisure.

Many in the capitalist class remain 'traditional' in outlook, emphasizing family connections and background, and placing great emphasis on the land and country pursuits, private schooling, 'old' and City money, and the centrality of royalty and the aristocracy. As high society and its official links with the state have waned, 'tradition' has come to be defined more closely in relation to the countryside and country values. The image of 'green and pleasant' villages and farms and of the country pursuits of those who live in and around them have come to embody English traditionalism.[10] Similarly, the traditionalism of the monarchy continues to legitimate the whole structure.

As in previous generations, the 'traditional' public schools and gentlemen's clubs are important elements in maintaining the cohesion of the capitalist class itself. They continue to provide and to reinforce a particular cultural outlook and, more importantly, a network of social connections which serve to increase the solidity of the class as a whole and to help in the reproduction of its members' privileges.

The London clubs of Pall Mall and the City were, of course, important supports of Society activities, providing a temporary residence for those who could not, or would not, afford the maintenance of a town house of their own. Although they never really recovered this role after the Second World War, they continued to provide a place of informality and sociability where economic and political activities could be discussed and deals struck. The capitalist class, no longer organized around an all-pervasive upper circle, was in even greater need of the kind of informal mechanism of integration and cohesion which was offered by club membership.

Lunchtime and evening meetings over a drink or a meal at the club have been frequent and important sources of information for those involved in business and politics. As centres for meetings and intrigue, however, the clubs have probably become a little less important than formerly. City institutions and other large enterprises have all expanded their internal catering facilities for directors and senior executives, and the 'working lunch' in the executive dining room has replaced many lunch-time club meetings. For many purposes, however, the 'neutral ground' of the club remains an important venue for meetings and discussions. Despite their reduced role, the clubs remain important as centres of informal interaction, sources of business and political information, and places for pursuing job and career opportunities.

Most important of the clubs in the post-war period have been the Reform and the Travellers, which are especially popular among senior civil servants, the smaller dining clubs such as Boodle's, Brooks's, Pratt's, The Beefsteak, Buck's, and White's, the university and service clubs, political clubs such as the Carlton, and the National Liberal and, at the hub of London clubland, the Athenaeum, which draws on all areas of politics, the civil service, and the City (See figure 5.1).

For many people, however, club membership is simply a necessary badge of status and acceptance, a sign that they are the 'right' kind of person. Many executive capitalists, for example, will collect club memberships but may rarely visit the clubs. To apply – and to be accepted – for club membership is a sign of secure social status, and to receive an offer of sponsorship in a membership application is a sign of recognition by those already secure in their status. To have a full collection of membership cards, like having a wallet full of credit cards, is a sign of membership in the upper circles. This status can be publicly displayed by listing club memberships in *Who's Who* and similar biographical directories, but such a person will often have better places to spend much of his time. As one commentator has said: 'Why lunch at the Carlton or the Reform when you can go to Langan's Brasserie?'[11]

The public schools were, of course, the other major support of the Victorian upper circle,[12] a role they continued to play to the full until the First World War. So long as the capitalist class was structured around an established upper circle, the public schools could simply produce the gentlemen that the families of the upper circle demanded – men capable of running the national society and playing their part in Society. As this upper circle became merely one among a number of overlapping upper circles, the public schools became less closely tied to the principles and processes of high society.

But educational changes take many years to make themselves felt in the structure of adult careers. During the 1930s there were still a great many prominent men in the state elite who had attended public schools in the Victorian period, the majority of them having completed their education in the 1870s and 1880s. The 'old boys' of the pre-1914 generations were still building their careers in business, politics, and the other leading institutions of British society. Their numbers had declined considerably by the mid-1950s, and many of the old boys in the state elite at this time had completed their education after 1914.

The 1944 educational reforms, carried through at the behest of the Labour party within the war-time coalition government, set up state-financed grammar schools in an attempt to open up educational opportunities and to create a meritocracy. These reforms had the paradoxical result of strengthening the public schools. Faced with the threat of greater competition for jobs from the sons and daughters of the middle and working classes, members of the capitalist class came to recognize more forcibly than before the benefits which their children could gain from a private education. As a result, the public schools underwent expansion: the number of pupils in private education rose by 20 per cent in the years following the reform of state education.

The pre-1944 grammar schools, private schools outside the circle of the top public schools, had all been thoroughly imbued with the public school ethos, and there was considerable career mobility

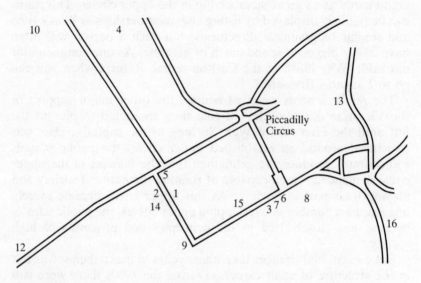

Clubs ranked by fees	Founded	Address
1 Boodle's	1762	St James's St, SW1
2 Brooks's	1764	St James's St, SW1
3 Reform	1836	Pall Mall, SW1
4 Buck's	1919	Clifford St, W1
5 White's	1693	St James's St, SW1
6 Athenaeum	1824	Pall Mall, SW1
7 Travellers'	1819	Pall Mall, SW1
8 Turf	1868	Carlton House Terr., SW1
9 Carlton	1832	St James's St, SW1
10 Savile	1868	Brook St, W1
11 City of London	1832	Old Broad St, EC2
12 Cavalry and Guards	1893	Piccadilly, W1
13 Beefsteak	1876	Irving St, WC2
14 Pratt's	1841	Park Place, SW1
15 Army and Navy	1837	Pall Mall, SW1
16 National Liberal	1882	Whitehall Place, SW1

The clubs are ranked in approximate order of their annual subscriptions. All except the City of London Club are shown by number on the sketch map.

Figure 5.1 Principal London clubs

for teachers between the grammar schools and the public schools. Grammar school boys who entered the state elite in the period between the First World War and 1944 carried this ethos with them. Directly and indirectly, therefore, the public school outlook remained a major influence among the upper circles throughout the twentieth century. Indeed, the last of the immediate pre-war generation of public and grammar school boys will not reach the official age of retirement until 1991. Those who attended the post-war grammar schools, still influenced by the outlook inherited from their predecessors, are still making their careers and have, until very recently, held only junior positions in the state elite.

The leading public schools – the so-called Clarendon schools, which had been identified as the leaders by the Clarendon Commission in the 1860s – were, in alphabetical order, Charterhouse, Eton, Harrow, Merchant Taylors, Rugby, St Paul's, Shrewsbury, Westminster and Winchester.[13] Alongside these were such other leading schools as Ampleforth, Felsted, Fettes, Haileybury, Loretto, Marlborough, Oundle, Radley, Sherborne, Stowe, and Wellington. (See table 5.1). The public schools collectively take just 5 per cent of the school population, and a half of these pupils are themselves the sons of former public schoolboys. Over a third of public schoolboys go on to university, overwhelmingly Oxford or Cambridge.

For the first half of the century Eton and Harrow had vied for top place among the public schools, but in the post-war world Eton was predominant. Eton was the richest of all the public schools, and its leading figures were, both officially and informally, at the heart of the capitalist class. The chairman of the board of governors of Eton, the Provost, was a Crown appointment, and other governors were directly appointed by Oxford and Cambridge Universities, the Royal Society, and the Lord Chief Justice. In its time it has produced twenty Prime Ministers.

Comprehensive reform in the 1960s and the growing tide of criticism of the 'elitism' of the public schools put them on the defensive for a while, but the abolition of the grammar schools re-invigorated them. Applications for entry increased and a number of the older grammar schools opted for private status. Although Eton's predominance slipped with increased competition from the other public schools, it and Winchester continued to provide entrants to the top levels of business and the state. Banking, diplomacy, and the Guards remained among the most important careers for Old Etonians, but they were to be found throughout politics, the civil service, and industry. In 1983, Old Etonians were to be found as

Table 5.1 *Public schools and their fees (1990)*

Leading schools

School	Annual boarding fees (£)
Ampleforth	7,830
Charterhouse	8,700
Eton	8,496
Harrow	8,850
Marlborough	8,100
Rugby	7,575
Shrewsbury	8,100
Westminster	7,950
Winchester	8,658

First-rate schools

School	Fees (£)	School	Fees (£)
Bedford	6,759	Malvern	8,085
Bradfield	8,250	Millfield	7,365
Bryanston	8,600	Oundle	8,550
Cheltenham	8,160	Radley	8,250
Clifton	8,310	Repton	7,110
Downside	7,206	St, Paul's	7,901
Fettes	7,455	Sedbergh	7,620
Gordonstoun	7,776	Sherborne	8,400
Haileybury	7,500	Stonyhurst	7,413
Highgate	6,810	Tonbridge	8,100
King's Canterbury	7,350	Uppingham	8,550
Lancing	7,191	Wellington	5,190

*The classification of the schools comes from T. Heald, *Networks* (Hodder and Stoughton, London, 1983).

the Governor of the Bank of England, the Chief of the Defence Staff, the editor of *The Times*, the head of the Home Civil Service, and the head of the Foreign Service. The heads of the top 200 wealthy families of 1990, discussed in the previous chapter (see table 4.3), included 35 Old Etonians and 25 men who had been officers in the Brigade of Guards.[14] Eton remained highly selective in its recruitment from the higher circles, though rather less self-recruiting than before: in 1961, 60 per cent of its pupils were the sons of Old Etonians, but by 1981 this figure had fallen to 43 per cent. In a larger sample of 31 public schools in the same year, the average proportion of pupils whose fathers had attended the same school was 18 per cent.[15]

The main continuing significance of the public schools lies in the role played by their 'old boy networks' in class reproduction. This network of connections and contacts, rooted in a similarity of social background and experience, provides the basis for a myriad of other informal contacts and connections. The importance of such networks of connections is that 'As society becomes more complex and the circles pull apart, so the people who can make connections between them become more useful as the fixers, the lubricants and brokers between one sphere and another.'[16]

I argued in the previous chapter that there has been a partial separation of the mechanisms of class reproduction from those of capital reproduction. The capitalist class no longer owes its privileges and advantages exclusively to inherited access to entrepreneurial locations. In the system of impersonal capital the recruitment of executive and finance capitalists depends upon the possession of educational credentials and other attributes deemed relevant to the performance of these tasks. The public schools play an important role in the acquisition of educational credentials. Members of the capitalist class can use their wealth to purchase a privileged education for their children, so ensuring that they are well placed in the educational race and stand a much enhanced chance of attending the universities of Oxford and Cambridge. It is the degrees of these universities which are still regarded by those who recruit executives and directors as being most appropriate for a career in business. Wealthy families are able to convert their wealth into the 'cultural assets' of the educational system, which can then be reconverted into enhanced economic opportunities and prospects for wealth accumulation.[17]

But entry to capitalist locations depends not simply on educational credentials; it depends also on other, less formal attributes which are rooted in upper-circle background and public schooling. The success of members of capitalist-class households in entering capitalist locations depends, to a substantial extent, on the social assets inherent in attendance at the 'right' school or college and which are manifest in comportment, speech, and dress. The 'old boy network' builds and reinforces these class attributes and provides people with the contacts and connections needed to improve their career prospects. When being considered for appointment or promotion, they find that the majority of those who are involved in the process of selection have themselves been through the same system and

Table 5.2 *The Old Boy network*

School	Rank		% of boys entering Oxford or Cambridge	
	1864	1955	1864	1955
Winchester	2	1=	45	57
Rugby	3	1=	41	57
Marlborough	14	3	24	53
Westminster	8	4	28	45
Clifton	*	5	–	41
Charterhouse	12	6	25	40
Shrewsbury	1	7	50	40
Ampleforth	*	8	–	37
Eton	6	9	33	35
Downside	*	10	–	35
Harrow	4	11	36	33
Tonbridge	16	12	19	30
Univ. Coll. Sch.	*	13	–	29
Oundle	8	14	–	27
Whitgift	*	15	–	27
Manchester	19	16	14	26
Radley	10	17	26	26
Birmingham, King Edward's	20	18	14	25
Bryanston	*	19	–	24
Wellington	*	20	–	23
St Paul's	11	22	25	23
Bradfield	7	23	29	22
Merchant Taylors'	17	28	17	20
Uppingham	13	30	25	19
Repton	5	31	35	18
Rossall	18	44	16	9
Bromsgrove	9	†	26	–
Brighton	15	†	19	–

Source: T. J. H. Bishop, *Winchester and the Public School Elite*, (Faber & Faber, London, 1957), Table 2, pp. 124–5.
The table shows the proportion of boys from each school gaining entry to either Oxford or Cambridge. Schools are ranked according to these figures, and schools appearing in the top 20 for either year are included. The data labelled '1864' relate to the period 1864–67.
* Not in top 20 of 1864–7.
† Not in the top 50 of 1955.
– % not known.

have come to accept its features as ensuring the normal and natural attributes of the 'right man' (*sic*) for the job. Miliband recognized that this same process operates in the state elite: 'Those who control and determine selection and promotion . . . are likely to carry in their minds a particular image of how a high ranking civil servant or military officer ought to think, speak, behave and react; and that image will be drawn in terms of the class to which they belong.'[18]

Without any need for a consciously intended bias in recruitment, the established 'old boys' sponsor the recruitment through their networks of contacts of each new generation of old boys. (See table 5.2). The public schools and Oxbridge colleges are the foundations of these networks which interconnect the various upper circles. Membership of the principal London clubs reinforces these connections by providing a venue for informal meetings among the old boys who may meet in other business and political contexts and by providing opportunities for pursuing careers and interests. Useem has argued that club membership is especially important for those at an early stage in their careers. For those who lack multiple directorships or are not yet involved at the centre of the major business organizations, 'participation in the club world doubles the probability of serving on a public board'.[19]

There exists a capitalist class with an *inner circle* of finance capitalists in Britain today, but these people are not the basis of an *upper circle* of status superiors. They are involved to varying degrees, and in varying ways, in the intersecting upper circles which have replaced high society at the top of the status hierarchy. It is in and through the informal social networks which connect these upper circles that class reproduction is ensured.

6 Is there still a Ruling Class?

Britain does still have a capitalist business class, rooted in industrial, commercial and landed property and occupying a position of high status. The privileges of this class are legitimated through a framework of 'traditional' norms and values, and the practices and processes of this status system are central to the mechanisms of class reproduction. But is the capitalist class still a ruling class? The concept of a ruling class, I have argued, is far from straightforward. In Chapter 2 I introduced a number of ideas which can help to evaluate the meaning and relevance of this concept. Before it is possible to answer the question 'Is there still a ruling class?', those ideas must be reviewed and elaborated.

Power Elites and the Ruling Class

The state elite comprises the positions of authority at the head of the leading institutions of the state. From this standpoint, all societies with a state have, by definition, a state elite and a political elite. It is for this reason that, for many commentators, the claims of classical elite theory have been seen as trivial. To claim that all societies have a political elite is not to claim very much at all. But there is far more to be learned from the elite theorists than this. While all societies with a state do, indeed, have a political elite, not all societies will have a *power elite*. The assertion that a particular society has a power elite is far from trivial, as it involves definite and contestable claims about the actual exercise of power. The occupants of positions of authority within the state elite comprise a power elite only where they are recruited from a power bloc. A power bloc, it will be recalled, is an alignment of social groups having some similarity in social background and experience and which is able to monopolize positions of authority within the state elite over a sustained period.

But to demonstrate the existence of a power elite is still only half the task, as power elites vary according to the cohesion and the class basis of the power bloc whith dominates the state elite. In figure 6.1 is a typology of power elites, defined by the dimensions in terms of which they may vary.[1] The first dimension in this typology measures the degree of cohesion and integration which the power bloc is able to achieve. This may vary from the situation where all sectors of the state elite are filled by those from a similar background to that where distinct clusters of positions are recruited from particular sections of the power bloc. The second dimension measures the class basis of the power bloc, and this may vary from the extreme of a highly restricted bloc, in which one particular class is dominant, to those situations involving more extended recruitment and where there is a broader balance of classes.

The social character and class base of the power elite varies in each of the situations defined in the typology. Rule by an *exclusive power elite* exists where the power bloc is drawn from a restricted and highly uniform social background and so is able to achieve a high level of solidarity. Rule by an *inclusive power elite*, on the other hand, exists where a solidaristic power bloc is not dominated by any particular class. While both cases involve the identification

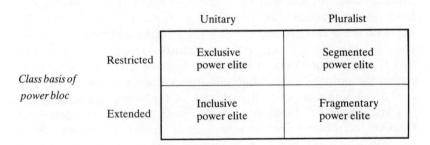

Figure 6.1 Forms of power elite

of a power elite with a high degree of solidarity and self-consciousness, they differ in terms of the restrictions which exist on membership of the power elite.

Rule by *segmented power elite* exists where the power bloc is divided into a number of separate and distinct fractions and has a relatively low level of overall cohesion, despite the fact that all fractions are drawn from the same restricted pool. In such a situation, competition between elements within the power elite will be strong. Rule by a *fragmentary power elite*, on the other hand, occurs where the power bloc has very little solidarity and cohesion, and where the basis of recruitment is somewhat wider. The relatively broad base of recruitment means that the various sections within the power elite constitute a pluralistic diversity of competing groups. In this situation, the concept of power elite becomes an almost abstract category to describe the competing, countervailing groups that participate in the exercise of power.

To describe a society as having a power elite, therefore, leads to the further stage of describing the particular form which is taken by this power elite. While each of these forms may be compatible with the existence of a ruling class, the nature of class rule and the extent to which the state may be expected to operate in the interests of the capitalist class will differ from case to case.

The classical Marxian view of the ruling class assumed the existence of a highly exclusive power elite: the state machinery was supposed to be dominated by a single class with a high level of class consciousness and solidarity. Pluralistic critics of this view, however, have rejected both aspects of this view. They have argued that the basis of recruitment to the political elite is far wider than the Marxists assume, and that its cohesion is also far less.[2] Miliband, I have shown, adopts an unorthodox Marxist position mid-way between these two extremes. While recognizing that positions within the state elite are not monopolized exclusively by the capitalist class and that there are certain important lines of division and conflict within the political elite, Miliband argues that these differences are contained within an overall similarity of outlook and background.

Underlying the dimension of the restricted or extended class basis of recruitment are the strategies of *closure* and *incorporation* through which the power bloc defines itself. Closure is a process through which a social group is able to secure the backing of the state and of the overall framework of law to establish certain privileges from which others are excluded and through which they

are able to ensure that the enjoyment of these privileges is closed
to outsiders.

Parkin has argued that the formal criteria of access and entry to
positions of privilege which are adopted in various societies – criteria
such as the 'rights' and 'obligations' attached to lineage, property,
or education – involve powerful processes of collective exclusion.[3]
Whole groups are excluded from such positions because their members are held to possess or to lack particular attributes. Positions
within the state elite, for example, may be restricted to those who
were born into recognized aristocratic families. Collective exclusion
can also occur when positions are formally 'open' to all through
competitive entry, examinations, and educational credentials. This
is the case, for example, where the members of a particular class
monopolize the 'cultural capital' which enables them to be more
successful than others in the educational race. Through their families
of birth, they acquire the cultural qualities, attributes and skills –
for example, those of language, literacy, and aesthetic enjoyment
– which are embodied in and reinforced by the educational system.
Classes which lack these inherited cultural assets are disadvantaged
in the educational system, and so a formal system of competitive
entry to elite positions will actually result in the exclusion of these
classes in favour of the other.[4] As I have shown in the previous
chapter, the public school system has, for a long time, operated in
just such a way to privilege the classes of the power bloc.

A successful monopoly of power may also depend upon the
continuing efforts of the members of the power bloc to maintain a
degree of closure while adopting a strategy of incorporation. In
these circumstances, the power bloc or its dominant group seeks to
maintain its dominance by enlarging the power bloc through the co-
optation of the leading elements of a rival group. In this way, it is
hoped that the opposition of the incorporated group will be defused.
Incorporation of wider social groups need not undermine the monopoly of the dominant class if those who are incorporated can be
relied upon to acquiesce in or to actively support the dominance of
those who have co-opted them. Indeed, a strategy of incorporation
will generally be followed because the dangers from continuing to
exclude a group are greater than those which would arise from their
incorporation in the existing power bloc.

It is in this context that a distinction between a power bloc and
an electoral bloc must be made. While the power bloc consists of
an alignment of social groups which actively participate in the

exercise of state power, an electoral bloc comprises the wider alignment of social groups which supports and sustains the power bloc
in electoral competition. An electoral bloc gives continued long-
term support to the political party or parties of the power bloc in
parliamentary and local elections, though its members are themselves outside the power bloc. Thus, challenging groups can be
incorporated into either the power bloc or the electoral bloc. Leading elements within the power bloc may, for example, seek to
incorporate potentially threatening social groups into an electoral
bloc, while continuing to exclude them from real participation in
state power.[5] Of particular importance in building an electoral bloc
are the values and ideas which can be encouraged among those
within the electoral bloc. Deferential attitudes among the working
class, for example, allow a stable electoral bloc to be built by
members of the dominant classes without there being any danger
that those who are incorporated will seek to gain entry to the power
bloc.

Practices of closure and incorporation maximize the cohesion of
the power bloc itself by emphasizing its separation from subordinate
groups outside the bloc. But this is not to say that relations within
the power bloc are egalitarian. I have emphasized that a power bloc
is an alignment of groups with differing life chances and conflicting
interests. These groups stand in relations of dominance and subordination to one another and, except in those rather unusual situations
where it is recruited exclusively from a single social group, a power
bloc will be organized around the balance of power and interests
among its constituent forces.

If a power bloc is to persist for any time, it must attain what
has sometimes been described as the three C's of consciousness,
coherence, and 'conspiracy'.[6] that is to say, the power bloc must
evolve some awareness of common interests and concerns, it must
achieve some degree of solidarity and cohesion, and its leading
members must be capable of pursuing some kind of coordinated
policy of action to further these interests. Those who are the occupants of similarly structured positions will, indeed, share certain
interests, but the achievement of a degree of coordination in their
actions in pursuit of these interests depends upon their becoming
conscious of these interests. It is only on this basis that the members
of the power bloc can achieve any consensus over policy goals and,
thereby, seek to influence successfully the direction of policy-making
in their interests.

Insights into the processes involved in this area can be gained from the work of C. Wright Mills on the power elite in the contemporary United States. This power elite, he argued, was recruited from the 'higher circles' of American society – it came from the privileged upper circles of those who 'know one another, see one another socially and at business, and so, in making decisions, take one another into account'. They are, Mills argued, 'involved in a set of overlapping "crowds" and intricately connected "cliques"'.[7] Their shared background and community of interaction among the upper circles is the basis of their shared understandings and their recognition of common interests, and it is the basis on which they are able to formulate a self-conscious awareness of what they have in common with one another:

> In so far as the power elite is composed of men [*sic*] of similar origin and education, in so far as their careers and their styles of life are similar, there are psychological and social bases for their unity, resting upon the fact that they are of similar social type and leading to the fact of their easy intermingling.[8]

The crucial bases of this group consciousness within the upper circles, argued Mills, are informal rather than formal. It is through communal solidarity and interaction rooted in family, schooling, clubs, and similar face-to-face milieux that the interests which they derive from their involvements in the larger and more impersonal structures of society are moulded. Economic and political interests – class interests – are shaped through informal interaction in small groups and through the networks of social relations through which they are connected. It is through similar upbringing and a continuing informal interaction that the members of the power elite are able to establish a degree of cohesion and social closure and so can sustain a policy consensus amongst themselves.

On this basis, and under certain circumstances, they are able to achieve high levels of coordination in their business practices and in pursuing shared policy preferences. Domhoff has pointed to the particularly important role played by what he terms 'consensus-seeking' and 'policy-planning' organizations, which are able to build a policy consensus for concerted action on the basis of the social cohesion established through patterns of informal interaction.[9] These bodies are: 'organisations created, financed, and directed by members of the ruling class for purposes of discussion and research on specific policy issues. They are one of the major means by which members of the ruling class come to agreement on such important topics as foreign policy, economic policy, welfare policy, population policy, and conservation policy.'[10]

These, then, are the mechanisms through which a power elite and its associated power bloc may be sustained and enabled to exercise their power. On this basis, the meaning of the concept of 'ruling class' may be restated. A ruling class exists when there is both political domination and political rule by a capitalist class. This requires that there be a power bloc dominated by a capitalist class, a power elite recruited from this power bloc, and in which the capitalist class is disproportionately represented, and that there are mechanisms which ensure that the state operates in the interests of the capitalist class and the reproduction of capital. In this sense, I shall show, Britain does still have a ruling class.

The Changing Anatomy of Political Rule

The old society of the eighteenth century was undoubtedly led by a ruling class. Positions in the state elite were monopolized by an exclusive power elite recruited from a power bloc composed of capitalist interests and of those whose propertied interests were tied to the social structure of agrarian capitalism. Within this power bloc, it was the capitalist class of patrician landowners which stood predominant. During the course of the nineteenth century this alignment of power began to alter. The exclusion of manufacturing capitalists from the power bloc and their alliance with professional and clerical workers looked for a time as if it would lead to the formation of a rival 'middle class' power bloc. Though achieving some sway in the local branches of the state machinery, however, this rival power bloc never fully flowered and did not become a major rival on the national political scene.

As a result, the tendency towards the formation of a segmented power elite, divided between the 'middle classes' and the group that Marx described as 'the guardians of Old England' was weak. The manufacturing capitalists, eventually, acquiesced in the continued national sway of the landed class, which increasingly sought to incorporate the more powerful elements of the middle class. Nineteenth-century Britain saw a gradual fusion of interests at the political level which matched the increasing integration of class interests at the economic level. There was little sign of any desire to create a substantially more inclusive power elite, despite the incorporation of some of the wealthier middle classes in the power bloc and, in a very few cases, the power elite. The bulk of the middle classes and the higher levels of the working classes were restricted to the extensive electoral bloc which underpinned the sway of the power bloc. The result was the creation of a new exclusive power elite, rooted in the new capitalist business class and supported by a power bloc which included professional middle-class interests and which had the cultural and electoral support of the wider middle classes and skilled artisans.

The form taken by the power elite of the late nineteenth and early twentieth century has been described as an 'establishment': an all-pervasive social and political force dominating all parts of the state apparatus and which was drawn from the highly restricted social background of the upper circle.[11] The reformed public schools and the traditional universities of Oxford and Cambridge were the foundation of an old boy network which was the key mechanism through which positions in the state elite were filled. At the heart of this establishment lay the Conservative party, which, as the Liberals became more closely identified with economic intervention and political reform, came to be seen as the natural party of property and business. Under Disraeli, the electoral bloc which had sustained the establishment was extended to include 'affluent' male manual workers, and the party became the Imperial party of Queen, Empire, and 'One Nation'.

The persistence of the power of the establishment, which has dominated politics for much of the twentieth century, can be seen in the continuity of personnel and practices over the period. Disraeli, Salisbury, and Balfour, successive leaders of the Conservative party, headed an exclusive power elite of immense persistence. The third Marquess of Salisbury, a descendant of William Cecil (Lord Burghley) the Lord Treasurer to Elizabeth I, succeeded Disraeli in the Conservative party leadership and headed a succession of Conservative governments from the middle of the 1880s until past the turn of the century. Salisbury had previously been Secretary of State for Indian and for Foreign Affairs, and for much of his time in office he combined the post of Prime Minister with that of Foreign Secretary. He resigned in 1902 and died the following year. He was succeeded as Prime Minister by Arthur Balfour, who remained in office until 1905, when the government was brought down by a deep split in its ranks over Joseph Chamberlain's tariff policy. The Balfour government turned out to be the last Conservative administration before the social and political watershed of the First World War. Balfour's government was followed by a succession of Liberal

Plate 6.1 Arthur Balfour: Statesman. (Author).

governments, ending with the formation of Asquith's national coalition during the first year of the war. It is possible, therefore, to see the Balfour government, in retrospect, as embodying the final stage of nineteenth-century Conservatism. An examination of the government of 1905 and the wider power elite of which it was a part will provide a firm and clear baseline for studying the development of the establishment during the twentieth century.

The Prime Minister in 1905, Arthur James Balfour, headed a cabinet of 18 members, including his own brother Gerald. Despite the death of the great Lord Salisbury, the Cecil family influence remained strong: the two Balfours were nephews of the Marquess of Salisbury and Arthur Balfour had been sponsored by him early in his political career. The fourth Marquess, heir to his father and cousin of Balfour, sat in the cabinet, as did his brother-in-law Lord Selborne. There was, as there always had been, a large number of Cecil M.P.s in parliament. In the previous generation of the family

Lord Eustace Cecil, brother of the third Marquess, had been an M.P., as had Lord Eustace's brother-in-law. In the same generation as the Balfour's and Lord Selborne were the M.P.s Evelyn Cecil (son of Lord Eustace), and the fourth Marquess's brothers Lord Robert and Lord Hugh.

The Cecil connections were not limited to parliament. As well as being extensively involved in county affairs in various parts of the country, the third Marquess had been Chancellor of Oxford University, his son William had been Rural Dean of Hertford, and Lord Eustace had been a Lieutenant Colonel in the Coldstream Guards. There were further establishment connections through marriage: Lord Arthur Cecil had married an Austrian baroness, and Edward Cecil had married an admiral's daughter.

Apart from the direct kin of the Cecils, the Balfour cabinet included a number of other long-established landowning families: Lord Londonderry, who owned 50,400 acres, Lord Onslow, with 13,500 acres, and Lord Lansdowne, the Foreign Secretary, who owned 143,000 acres. In all, seven members of the House of Lords sat in the cabinet. A further three cabinet members were the sons of peers, and one was the grandson of a peer. Outside the cabinet were a further 30 ministers, including seven peers, eight baronets and knights, and numerous others from landowning and industrial families.

Many of the members of the Tory government had business interests, but only Austen Chamberlain, Chancellor of the Exchequer, came from a wealthy and established dynasty of industrialists – his family were prominent members of the Birmingham industrial world. Despite their close economic fusion with landowners, industrialists remained, at this time, rather more closely associated with the Liberal party, and it was Chamberlain's father, Joseph, who created the split in the Conservative party which was to end its long period in power. Outside the cabinet, in the wider ranks of the Conservative party in parliament, however, were large numbers of industrialists and men with interests which spanned the worlds of land, commerce, and industry.

The education of the Conservative government of 1905 took place in a very narrow range of institutions. The cabinet included eight Old Etonians and four other former public school boys – two from Rugby, one from Harrow, and one from Winchester. Fourteen cabinet ministers, more than two thirds of the total cabinet, had undergone a university education: nine at Oxford, four at Cambridge, and one at Dublin. These men were, furthermore, drawn from a small number of colleges, whose fellows and former members were able to sponsor the movement of their students into the state elite. Among the Oxbridge contingent there were four from Trinity College in Cambridge and four from University College at Oxford.

Industrialists in the wider society had largely accepted the hegemony of the values of the old landed class, and it was the Oxbridge colleges and the public schools which played a key role in moulding these values into a coherent outlook on social life. The colleges and the schools from which they recruited their students were at the heart of a system of sponsorship and recruitment through which the leading positions in the state elite were filled. This system of education ensured superior life chances for those who entered it, and it ensured that the power elite was replenished by a constant supply of new recruits who possessed the cultural attitudes and outlook appropriate for the continuation of the establishment and its 'traditional' social order.

If the 'traditional' landed outlook continued to dominate the heart of the state elite, it was even more strongly represented in its wider circles. As might be expected, the Royal Household was especially close to the world of the landed interest. The Keeper of the Privy Purse in 1905, Sir Dighton Probyn, was a retired general; the Lord Chamberlain, Lord Clarendon, was from a long established City and landowning family; and the Lord Steward, Lord Pembroke, was a major landowner in Wiltshire. The major areas of overseas official administration were held by men from a similar background: the Viceroy of India was Lord Curzon, and the Governor General of Canada was Lord Grey.

The army, the navy, the established church, and the civil and foreign service had all developed towards 'professional' administrative bureaucracies,[12] but despite the importance of professionalism and of technical competence, 'traditional' criteria of recruitment remained strong. Honorary positions of Field Marshal were, of course, held by members of the British and European Royal families (including Kaiser Wilhelm II and the Emperor Franz Josef), together with two peers and two knights, but the 21 generals on the active lists were just as restricted in their recruitment. The generals included 17 men with titles: four members of the British and foreign Royal families, three members of the House of Lords, one son of a peer, one baronet, and eight knights. The untitled generals were officers in the Royal Marines, rather than the more prestigious cavalry, artillery, and infantry regiments. Admirals of the Fleet and admirals, excluding four Royal admirals holding honorary rank, numbered

15, and these included ten knights and one peer. The 'career' element of rising through the officer ranks was rather stronger in the navy than in the army, though many of its senior officers came from old naval families which had provided recruits to the officer grades over the centuries. The Church of England, too, showed a strong reliance on recruitment from families with a tradition of service to the institution. The Archbishop of Canterbury in 1905, for example, was Randall Davidson, the son-in-law of a former Archbishop.

Not only were those from the titled world recruited to the upper realms of the state. It was also the case that titles were used to cement the cohesion of the power elite by strengthening the attachment of newcomers to the 'traditional' order of the establishment. In both branches of the military apparatus of the state there had emerged a tendency for the award of a knighthood to become the mark of political recognition given to those from the gentry who had achieved senior rank, and a similar process was in operation in the legal apparatus: all five of the Lord Justices in Appeal, for example, were knights. In the diplomatic and civil service this same pattern existed, as did the pattern of recruitment from establishment families. The ambassador to France in 1905, Sir Francis Bertie, was both the son and the son-in-law of an earl, while both the ambassador to Germany (Sir Frank Lascelles, cousin of the Earl of Harewood) and the Permanent Under Secretary at the Foreign Office (Sir Thomas Sanderson) were the sons of M.P.s and the grandsons of peers. Sir Edward Hamilton, joint Permanent Secretary at the Treasury, was the son of a bishop.

In the local branches of the state, a similar pattern could be found. The Lords Lieutenant of the counties came predominantly from established landowning families at the higher levels of the peerage, while commercial and industrial families found some county involvement in roles such as that of High Sheriff. On the recently established County Councils the representation of industrial interests alongside landowners was much stronger, as it was on the Quarter Sessions bench. In Norfolk, Essex, Northamptonshire, Northumberland, and Somerset, for example, the Lords Lieutenant in 1905 comprised four earls and a marquess. In the same counties, the High Sheriffs were drawn from commercial and industrial families. The High Sheriffs of Norfolk and Essex were Hugh Barclay and Thomas Buxton from the intermarried banking families associated with Barclays Bank, and the High Sheriff of Northamptonshire was a Rothschild. In Northumberland the High Sheriff was John

Milburn, a local industrialist, and in Somerset the position was held by Sir William Wills from the wealthy tobacco dynasty.

In all areas of the state elite in 1905, therefore, there was a considerable over-representation of capitalist class families with interests in industry, commerce and land, showing clearly the existence of an exclusive power elite. The members of this elite were tied together through both the *inter*-generational and the *intra*-generational 'circulation' of persons from one position and one branch to another. The power elite was characterized by high cohesion and closure.

The situation that I have described for 1905 is merely a snapshot picture of a continuing process of capitalist class political power. This power did not come to an end with the fall of the Conservative government in 1905. Members of the Liberal party and its 'national' coalition governments were also drawn from a similar, though rather more industrial background, and many areas of the state elite were unaffected by the change of government. In any case, the electoral and parliamentary decline of the Liberal party – it has never formed a government since the First World War – strengthened the position of the Conservative party as the 'establishment' party of property and business, the party of the capitalist business class. An accumulation of evidence from a whole series of studies has shown that, despite the changes which the capitalist business class has undergone in the course in the twentieth century, it has continued to dominate recruitment to the state elite.

This can be documented in all areas of the state. Guttsman's study of the cabinet showed that the proportion of cabinet ministers who were manufacturers, merchants, or bankers, or were from the wider professional middle classes remained constant, at a level of around a half of all cabinet posts, throughout the whole period from 1868 to 1955. There was, over this period, a rise in the number of 'working-class' ministers, predominantly during periods of Labour government, and this was almost exclusively at the expense of those whose class base was solely in landownership. The proportion of cabinet ministers with substantial personal landholdings was a half in the period between 1868 and 1916 and one quarter between 1916 and 1955.[13] This decline in the representation of personal landownership reflects the increasing fusion of landownership with other forms of property ownership within the capitalist class and the consequent decline of 'traditional' landownership as the basis of a distinct class segment. A study of the period since 1955 has shown that working-class membership of cabinets has declined, as

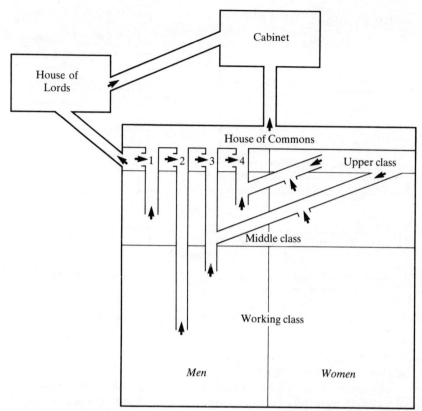

KEY: The parallelogram represents the entire electorate ranged hierarchically in social classes and split vertically into men and women. At the summit stands the political elite with four major channels of access opening into it: 1. the public schools; 2. trade union and Co-op sponsorship; 3. non-Oxbridge universities; 4. Oxbridge. The 'depth' of each channel is determined by which groups have general access to it — e.g. channel 4 (Oxbridge) affords predominant access to upper and middle class men, with minority access to women of the same or slightly higher average rank. It is, of course, entirely possible for elite entrants to traverse more than one channel — e.g. public school *and* Oxbridge.

Source: Modified from R. W. Johnson, 'The British Political Elite', *European Journal of Sociology* (1973). p. 42.

Figure 6.2   Routes into government

the Labour party has come to recruit more and more of its ministers from the professional middle classes. Conservative cabinets, on the other hand, have shown little change: the working class had achieved little representation at the top of the Conservative party. (See figure 6.3). The narrowly 'landed' interest has continued its gradual decline

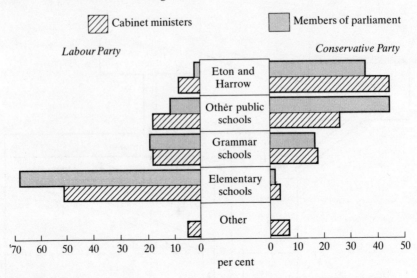

Source: W. G. Guttsman, *The British Political Elite* (MacGibbon & Kee, London, 1963), p. 96.

Figure 6.3   Educational background of M.P.s and the cabinet (1918–1955)

since the 1950s, and the predominance of business and the professions has been reinforced.[14]

Throughout the whole century or more since 1868, the proportion of cabinet ministers coming from a background of land, business and the professions has varied from 100 per cent at the beginning of the period to something over three quarters at its end. As shown in figure 6.3, the public schools and Oxbridge, also, continued to play their part in socializing the sons of the power elite and in enhancing their movement into positions similar to those held by their fathers.[15] The importance of public schooling in securing access to the state elite in recent years is apparent from the fact that virtually all cabinet members between 1951 and 1964 had been to public schools. By 1983, the public-school contingent within the cabinet had fallen slightly, to just below three quarters. Despite the growing significance among cabinet ministers of education outside the public schools, even within the Conservative party, an Oxbridge education remained a unifying force. Over three quarters of cabinet ministers in 1983 were from Oxford or Cambridge universities – exactly the same proportion as 30 years earlier. Two thirds of cabinet members in this year had attended both a public school and one of the two traditional universities.[16]

Throughout the 1950s and 1960s, around one third of cabinet members had been educated at one public school alone: Eton. Sampson reported that six of the 21 members of the Macmillan cabinet of 1959 were Old Etonians. This was the period in which Harold Macmillan described the growing affluence of British society in the immortal words 'never had it so good', and he underlined the point by referring to the quality of his cabinet: 'Mr Attlee had three Old Etonians in his cabinet. I have six. Things are twice as good under the Conservatives.'[17] Things had 'improved' even further by 1979, as Margaret Thatcher's first Conservative cabinet included seven Old Etonians, a quarter of its membership. As noted above, the overall figure for public-school background in the cabinet remained at three quarters in 1983.

This review of the changing anatomy of political rule began with a consideration of the Conservative cabinet of 1905. How does this compare with the Conservative cabinet of 1990? The 1990 cabinet had 23 members, headed by Margaret Thatcher. The most striking change, of course, is the fact that the cabinet was headed by a woman and that she had held this office for a record-breaking period of more than ten years. Mrs Thatcher had attended a local authority

Plate 6.2 The Thatcher Cabinet. 1979 Thatcher cabinet at 10 Downing Street. (Reproduced by kind permission of The Hulton Picture Company.)

grammar school in Lincolnshire, epitomizing the impression projected for her whole government of the self-made, meritocratic
middle classes who had replaced the old grandees of the Tory party.
In fact, she was one of only two members of her cabinet not to
have attended a fee-paying school. While many of the old ruling
families had, indeed, disappeared from the cabinet, private schooling remained the most important route to political success. The
cabinet included three Old Etonians (Geoffrey Hurd, Nicholas Ridley, and Lord Belsted), and old boys of Winchester, Rugby, Charterhouse, and Marlborough, as well as such prominent Scottish
schools as George Herriot's and George Watson's. A number of the
schools attended did, indeed, contain the words 'grammar school' in
their names, but this was, prior to the Butler Education Act, a
phrase that was used by many independent and fee-paying schools.
Nineteen of the members of the cabinet had attended a university:
eight at Oxford, eight at Cambridge, two at Edinburgh, and one at
St Andrew's. No provincial, red-brick universities were represented.
Colleges represented more than once in the cabinet were Balliol,
Emmanuel, and Trinity Hall.[18]

In the wider sphere of parliament also, the public schools
remained the crucial channels of access for members of the Conservative party. The number of former public school boys in parliament as Conservative M.P.s stood at 216 in 1951 and 243 after the
Conservative electoral victory of 1970: an increase from 68 per cent
to 74 per cent. Nineteen per cent of Conservative M.P.s in 1970
were Old Etonians. More than a half of Tory M.P.s over the whole
post-war period attended Oxford or Cambridge colleges, and almost
a half had attended both a public school and Oxbridge.[19]

The same situation holds outside government and parliament.[20]
Over the period since 1939, as shown in table 6.1, the top levels of
the civil service (the grades of under-secretary and above) experienced a marked decline in the proportion of recruits with a private
school background. The decline from the pre-war figure of more
than 90 per cent, however, was largely due to the war-time recruitment of large numbers of 'temporary' civil servants from outside
the normal circles of recruitment to meet the requirements of the
expanded warfare apparatus. Many of these recruits remained in
the civil service after the war, when the new 'welfare' ministries
began to expand. The earlier patterns of recruitment soon re-
established themselves, however, and the proportion with a public
or other fee-paying education began to creep up. By the 1960s, the
proportion had reached two thirds, the same as the proportion

Table 6.1 *Civil and foreign service recruitment (1939–1970)*

| | | % from private school or Oxbridge in: | | | |
		1939	1950	1960	1970
Top civil servants	Fee paying	90.5	59.9	65.0	61.7
	Oxbridge	77.4	56.3	69.5	69.3
Ambassadors	Fee paying	75.5	72.6	82.6	82.5
	Oxbridge	49.0	66.1	84.1	80.0

Top civil servants are here regarded as under-secretaries and above. Here and in
Table 6.2, the percentage figures are based on small numbers and it is appropriate
to use them only for broad comparisons.
Source: D. Boyd, *Elites and their Education*, NFER, (London, 1973) tables 4, 5,
13, and 14, pp. 80–1, 86–7.

recruited from Oxford or Cambridge. Not all who attended a public
school, of course, went on to Oxbridge, and the old universities
have been important channels of access to the upper levels of the
civil service for many middle-class grammar school boys. In the high
status and high profile areas of the diplomatic corps, the figures are
even higher. In the first half of the present century almost all
ambassadors to major countries had attended a public school, and
in the second half of the century the figure was still as high as four
fifths in 1960. The proportion recruited from Oxbridge showed a
marked increase over the post-war period, passing two thirds by
1950 and four fifths by 1970. In both the 1960s and the 1970s, over
a quarter of ambassadors had fathers who had been among the
prominent persons listed in *Who's Who*.

In the army, the proportion of top officers from a public-school
background increased over the century. At the turn of the century,
about one third of the generals and lieutenant generals had received
a public-school education, many of the others having been educated
'privately' at home. By the beginning of the Second World War,
this figure had increased to four fifths, and in 1971 it had reached
nine tenths. Table 6.2 shows that more than four fifths of those in
the rank of major general or above in 1970 had experienced a
public-school education, and a quarter had attended Oxford or
Cambridge, both of these figures showing a steady upward trend
over the post-war period. Public-school recruitment was less marked
in the navy and the RAF, though one third of those holding the
rank of rear admiral or above and two thirds of those of air vice-
marshal rank or above in 1970 had attended public schools. The

Table 6.2 *Military and judiciary recruitment (1939–1970)*

| | | % from private school or Oxbridge in: | | | |
		1939	1950	1960	1970
Top army	Fee paying	63.6	71.9	83.2	86.1
	Oxbridge	2.5	8.8	12.4	24.3
Top navy	Fee paying	19.8	14.6	20.9	37.5
	Oxbridge	–	–	–	–
Top air force	Fee paying	69.7	59.1	59.5	65.0
	Oxbridge	18.2	13.6	19.1	17.5
Top judiciary	Fee paying	84.4	86.8	82.5	83.5
	Oxbridge	77.8	73.6	74.6	84.6

Ranks included above are: army – major general and above; navy – rear admiral
and above; air force – air vice-marshal and above; judiciary – high court judges
and above. The numbers of naval officers attending university was so low that they
were not included in the calculation.
Source: As table 6.1: tables 6–9, 15–17, pp. 81–3, 88–90.

figures for naval officers are significantly higher if attendance at
Dartmouth – the navy's own 'public school' is included: the combined figure for private schools and Dartmouth in 1970 was 89 per
cent. Among high court judges, well over a half were from legal
families, and about one fifth were from peerage families. The
proportion who had attended private schools and Oxbridge
remained constant over the whole period, 1939–1970. Four fifths of
top judges in 1970 were from public schools – around two fifths
coming from Eton, Winchester, Harrow, and Rugby. In all areas
of the military and the top judiciary – with the exception of senior
RAF officers – over a quarter of office holders in 1960 had fathers
who had been listed in *Who's Who*.

This evidence on social background and recruitment shows clearly
the persistence of a power bloc dominated by the capitalist class. It
is important, however, to be clear about the nature of this evidence.
Studies which have shown a disproportionate representation of
public-school graduates in the various arms of the state elite in
Britain do not, in themselves, show that there is a capitalist class
monopolization of these positions, as many people from outside this
class attend public schools.

What these studies show is that people, from various classes, who
have experienced a public-school education are to be found in the
state elite in far greater numbers than would be expected if positions

were allocated more equitably. There is a systematic bias towards recruitment from the particular social background of business and the professions, and not simply from a background of property. Members of the capitalist class are, of course, disproportionately represented at the public schools, at Oxbridge, and within the state elite, but their power within the state operates through a wider power bloc which shares its characteristic outlook and values. While most men in the capitalist class may have experienced a public-school education, this experience and its distinctive outlook and habits are shared with members of certain other classes. Although 5 or 6 per cent of men have attended a public school, the proportion of those at the top levels of the service class who had done so was, in the mid-1970s, 35 per cent. The figure for members of the capitalist class is even higher than this – it was estimated that over 90 per cent of top-income recipients in 1953 were paying for their children's education.[21]

Similarly, studies of business representation in the state elite have shown that company directors and executives are disproportionately represented there. But the category of directors and executives includes many people who are not in the capitalist class, as it stretches from the top levels of business down through the *petty bourgeoisie* to middling salaried executives. These people of diverse class origins do experience, to a certain degree, a similar 'business background' and therefore, a similarity of outlook and behaviour. Their commitment to property and enterprise gives them common cause with the capitalist class and creates the basis for a community of interest. But the evidence on the over-representation of business and executive interests in the state elite, as with that on public school and Oxbridge attendance, indicates the importance of the larger power bloc in sustaining capitalist-class dominance.

Studies of social background affirm the existence of a power bloc: an alliance of classes rooted in the unifying features of distinct patterns of social background. An alignment of the capitalist business class, the entrepreneurial middle class and the service class, in a shifting balance, comprises the power bloc of Britain today. It is this particular pattern of alignment that Miliband and others have misleadingly described as a 'dominant class'. As should be clear by now, this terminology must be rejected in favour of one which recognizes the existence of a power bloc within which a capitalist business class holds a dominant position. It is from this power bloc that a power elite is formed to monopolize recruitment to the state elite.

It must not be assumed that the state is the mere 'instrument' of the capitalist class. It is rarely, if ever, the case that a whole class can achieve the kind of unity of action that would allow it to utilize the state machinery as a direct instrument of its preferred policies. Any analysis of state power must take account of divisions within the capitalist class and its sharing of power with members of other classes. Under some circumstances, members of the capitalist class may take a back seat within the power elite, relying on others to operate the state in a way that does not undermine its class interests. An increase in the number of positions held by people from the entrepreneurial middle class or the service class, for example, may be effective in maintaining the cohesion of an electoral bloc on whose support the continuation of capitalist-class representation within the state depends. Nor must it be assumed that this form of class dominance involves the adoption of a 'conspiratorial' approach to political matters on the part of the capitalist class – such an assumption would be patently ridiculous. Conspiracies do occur, of course, but they are limited to relatively small groups and they rarely have the kind of impact on affairs that many assume. It is simply necessary to recognize that the politically active members of the capitalist class, invariably a small minority, may come to some kind of awareness that their own intersts would be better served through broadening the base of the power elite – making it more inclusive – than by adopting a highly exclusive stance. Political parties are the crucial mechanisms through which strategies of dominance are formed. The Conservative party may be seen as having mobilized a power bloc based in industrial, commercial and landed capitalist interests, and extending into the managerial and professional middle classes. This has been the basis of political leadership during periods of Conservative government.

Over the course of the century, there have been important changes in the structure within which the power elite operates. The 'establishment', a 'traditional' alignment based around shared values and a similarity of background, continues to exist, but in only a very attenuated form of its old self. Its informal practices of cohesion and solidarity have been supplemented by more formal means of recruitment and political representation as state activity has become more centralized and interventionist. Formal organizations of capital – employers' organizations and business interest groups – have organized wider elements of the capitalist class outside the establishment, and have sought to represent business interests through more formal channels. As a result, the power elite is not so dominated by the establishment as it was at the turn of the century. As the establishment has weakened, so the state elite has been recruited from wider sections of the capitalist class and from the middle classes. It remains subject to capitalist-class domination, but formal mechanisms of interest representation are now a more important element in the exercise of political power.

At the same time, trades unions and the Labour party have sought to use similar formal channels to represent working-class interests and have, on occasion, been able to secure parliamentary majorities and to form governments which introduce people from a wider social background. The remainder of the state elite, however, has remained firmly dominated by the power bloc. Periods of Labour government can be seen as periods in which the power elite has been forced by electoral pressure to relinquish certain of the positions which it normally monopolizes. But its entrenched position in the non-elected parts of the state apparatus has enabled it to prevent Labour members from using their power to make any substantial alteration in the composition of the state elite as a whole. The Labour party has *governed*, but it has not *ruled*. Even less has it altered the pattern of class political *dominance*.[22]

The Structure of Political Domination

In order to demonstrate that the capitalist class actually stands in a position of political dominance, as well as being disproportionately represented in the pattern of political rule, it is necessary to explore the mechanisms through which this political domination can be achieved. The political dominance of a capitalist class, it will be recalled, consists in the state operating in such a way as to maintain the conditions of that class's economic dominance. To say that the state operates in the interests of a particular class is to refer to the class character of state power. It is to hold that what is done through the means of the state apparatus 'positively acts upon the (re-) production of the mode of producton, of which the class in question is the dominant bearer'.[23] A state operates in the interests of a capitalist class when its activities reinforce the conditions for the reproduction of that class and it fails to act in ways which undermine these conditions.

Reinforcement of the conditions of reproduction of a capitalist class involves, above all, the maintenance of the existing social relations through which the system of capitalist production is reproduced and through which the privileges of a capitalist class are perpetuated. But it may involve also the intensified application of these relations and their extension to new areas beyond the existing bounds of capitalist production. Conversely, the undermining of these conditions would involve restricting the scope of application of capitalist relations and, in extreme cases, suppressing or eliminating their conditions.[24] In more concrete terms, the reinforcement of the conditions of reproduction of the mode of production that sustains a capitalist class involves such things as guaranteeing the legal framework of property, company, and commercial law on which business activities depend, pursuing economic policies which are supportive of private profit and capital accumulation, and undertaking social policies supportive of the material advantages enjoyed by the capitalist class. The state is often the only organization capable of undertaking activities which are necessary for the reproduction of private capital but which cannot easily be provided by individual capitalist enterprises. Such important activities include the provision of health, welfare, education, and basic scientific research facilities, the planning and coordination of economic restructuring, and the establishment of the whole legal and disciplinary framework of internal and external order. The fact that such activities are undertaken is evidence that the state is operating in the interests of capitalist reproduction.

This is not to say that state policy needs to be solely concerned with advantaging the capitalist class. When the state's activities advantage several classes rather than simply the dominant class, it is still possible to speak of a ruling class, so long as these activities do not undermine the existing relations of production and continue, in the long term, to reinforce them. As Therborn says:

> *Rule by a single class* (or fraction thereof) will cover systems of state interventions ranging from that in which the state furthers or maintains the positions of one class alone, through that where a specific class has a *predominant* position in at least the state apparatus, to that where the state goes against the positions of a dominant class without furthering the positions of another, and without maintaining those of another economically dominant class (where one exists). The range stretches from the peak of power of a ruling class to the stage where, while still holding a monopoly of power, it is forced to retreat and yield concessions.[25]

The existence of a ruling class is not in the slightest undermined by the existence of a power bloc or by the making of concessions to its subordinate members. It becomes necessary to speak of a ruling alliance of classes rather than a ruling class *per se* only when the activities of the power elite controlling the state further, to an equivalent degree, the positions and opportunities of two or more classes, or where they systematically advantage a class in one area while disadvantaging them, to the advantage of another, in a different area.[26] For a ruling class to exist, therefore, it is simply necessary that the advantages derived by its partners in the power bloc are not made in such a way as to disadvantage systematically the dominant class and its conditions of reproduction. Redistribution of income and wealth, for example, may be undertaken in such a way that the life chances of certain groups are improved while the capitalist class remains significantly advantaged relative to the rest of the population. What is significant is that the capitalist class should benefit to a greater extent than any other group.

Numerous writers in the 'pluralist' tradition of political analysis have held that the political dominance of a class, if it exists in a society, will be manifest in its successfully securing decisions favourable to itself.[27] But the mechanisms of political domination involve not only – or even mainly – 'decisions', understood as particular, discrete acts of political will. They involve also what have been termed 'non-decisions': the 'bias' or 'structural selectivity' which is built into the normal routine operations of the state and which ensure that certain interests and issues never reach the point of decision.[28] As Westergaard and Resler argue: 'individuals or groups may have effective benefits of "power" without needing to exercise it in positive action . . . [There is] a passive enjoyment of advantage and privilege, obtained merely because of "the way things work" and because those ways are not exposed to serious challenge.'[29]

There is little point in searching for class 'victories' in a series of contested decisions – few such decisions have been necessary. A key element in capitalist-class domination, for example, is the state's role in guaranteeing the pattern of proprietary control in business on which the capitalist class depends. This is rooted in the framework of property, company, and commercial law and in the principles of private ownership and free contract which underpin this framework. This system of law and its underlying values were formulated and enacted over an extremely long period and were firmly entrenched by the end of the nineteenth century.[30] There have, since then, been periodic extensions and elaborations of these laws, often highly technical and detailed, but the basic framework and principles have never been renegotiated through the decision-making apparatus of the state. No attempt has been made to bring to the point of decision the reversal of the original enactments or the rejection of the underlying principles. The matters have never been brought into the decision-making arena, even during periods of Labour government.

Over time, therefore, a structure of selectivity is built into the state as a result of its past policies and practices. A set of established practices is built into the administrative routines of the various branches of the state and these are sustained by the personnel, at all levels, who are recruited and promoted on the basis of their ability to follow these established routines.[31] This bias creates a predisposition for the state to act in a way consistent with its past practices.

Gramsci argued that class domination depended upon the establishment of a cultural hegemony, a process through which a particular way of seeing and evaluating the world was diffused and widely accepted among the population as 'natural'. Building on this argument Wesolowski has stressed that a structural selectivity can be ensured in state activities wherever the conditions of continued class dominance are formulated in a system of ideas which are accepted by the members of the state elite. The existence of this limited cultural hegemony ensures that state operations are biased towards the class whose interests are expressed in these ideas. A high degree of consensus among the political rulers around such a legitimating set of ideas helps to ensure that they will not willingly undermine the conditions of class dominance. Under these circumstances state policy will be supportive of the capitalist class, and the class background of the political rulers is of far less significance in ensuring class dominance.[32]

But this is true only if there is a perfect consensus around the basic principles of capitalist dominance and a thorough exclusion of alternative ideas. Alternative ideas, of course, do not necessarily run counter to the requirements of capitalist dominance, but the hegemony argument clearly requires that there be some limitation on the range of ideas current within the state elite. Unless this is the case, the state will be beset by dissension and rivalries between and within its various branches, and it will be unlikely to pursue an unambiguously 'capitalist' policy. Thus, Poulantzas sees ideology as an 'internal cement' which prevents the divisions and rivalries of the various branches of the state from leading to complete disunity.[33] Miliband adds that the dominant ideology comprises 'a cluster of common ideological and political positions and attitudes, common values and perspectives', which ensure that differences of view within the power elite 'occur within a specific and fairly narrow conservative spectrum'.[34]

Abercrombie and his colleagues have argued that, compared with earlier centuries, a dominant ideology has become a weaker force in uniting the capitalist class. There is rather more diversity in the ideas and meanings into which the members of this class are socialized. They argue, for example, that rights to the personal ownership and transfer of property are less strongly emphasized than are the needs of profit and capital accumulation, reflecting the decline of personal possession and the concomitant growth of the system of impersonal capital.[35] This has allowed, for example, an enhanced interventionist role for the state to develop in the promotion of capital accumulation, a role which would have been seen as an infringement on the rights of the property owner in an earlier period. Despite this, there has been no significant challenge to private ownership and the system of property through which impersonal capital is structured. Nationalization of business enterprises has been limited and, in many cases, short-lived. Those enterprises which have remained in public ownership over a long period have been those which require state support for their continued operations and which would be unprofitable in private hands. The trend of the last ten years or so has not only reversed much nationalization, through the policy of privatization, it has also re-invigorated the ideological basis of private property and free enterprise through an emphasis on the creation of an 'enterprise culture'.

The extent to which a dominant ideology exists among the members of the state elite depends upon how such ideas are formulated and transmitted. The central mechanisms involved here are those of socialization within the family and the school, and the subsequent reinforcement of acquired ideas through informal interaction later in life. A capitalist class is far more likely to be sustained by a compliant state elite if it can form a power bloc rooted in a relatively uniform pattern of socialization. Schooling and family upbringing can establish a bedrock of shared meanings which become the basis of a legitimating framework of ideas. The public schools and the grammar schools attended by those from capitalist-, entrepreneurial-, and service-class backgrounds are crucial mechanisms in the creation of this set of ideas within the power bloc. Through frequent informal and formal interaction among members of the power elite, these ideas congeal into the 'internal cement', the consensus which binds them together.

If these same ideas can be disseminated to the lower levels of the middle classes and sections of the working class, a stable electoral bloc is far easier to build. Parkin, for example, has stressed the role of deferential and aspirational meaning systems among subordinate classes as supports of a dominant meaning system which represents the 'perceptions and advantages of the relatively privileged'.[36] This wider dissemination was central to Gramsci's original idea of a cultural hegemony. To establish a cultural hegemony, the members of a power bloc must colonize certain salient institutions which lie outside the state elite itself, but which are central to the formation and maintenance of a cultural consensus. Of particular importance are the media of mass communication and the Church of England, through which dominant ideas and meanings are disseminated. Because of their close involvement in the process of legitimation, many writers have treated these institutions as if they were parts of the state apparatus itself, including their leading members within the state elite.[37] For the reasons I set out in Chapter 2, I do not regard this as correct. The church and the mass media stand outside the state apparatus, and they play a separate and independent role in the structure of power. Those who doubt the continuing relevance of the church should consider the great attention that the Thatcher government has given to the statements of church leaders whom they see as undermining the tenets of the enterprise culture. By filling the leading positions in these institutions, members of the power bloc solidify the hold of the cultural hegemony over the occupants of the state apparatus as well as the wider society. The degree of consensus in any society, of course, is unlikely to be perfect. The possibility of discontent and challenge is always present and so further mechanisms of political domination are necessary if a class is to continue to rule.

The economic constraints which are faced by the state are, perhaps, of greatest importance. A modern state must raise its revenue from taxation and from borrowing. These fiscal constraints mean that the state depends on the existence of a profitable sector of private business and so must support social policies which will be directly or indirectly supportive of capital accumulation.[38] It can engage in other policies only if they do not seriously undermine the private profitability which allows the operations of private capitalism to continue to generate sufficient tax revenue or borrowing capacity. A particular government may, of course, choose to ignore these constraints. In this case, it will find that declining profitability undermines its ability to carry through its policies. The Labour government of 1974–79 found that international agencies such as the International Monetary Fund can impose even tighter restrictions on government policy as a condition for a 'rescue' operation under such circumstances. An expanding role for the state in the economy and a rising level of tax revenue will not threaten the reproduction of capitalist relations if they are not directed at the promotion of alternative relations or the systematic advantaging of subordinate classes. State revenues, for example, are generally transferred back to the private sector through subsidies and state purchases of goods and services and through direct transfer to households which spend their enhanced income on privately produced consumption goods.[39] As the British economy has become heavily tied into the global structure of the world economic system, so these constraints have become tighter. The scope for autonomy on the part of the state has, accordingly, diminished.

The cultural and economic constraints will tend to be mutually re-inforcing. Cultural consensus within the power bloc ensures that there will be, at minimum, a willingness among members of the power elite to continue to adopt fiscal policies based on the existence of a thriving sector of private enterprise. And the fiscal constraints will tend to ensure that policy preferences remain in line with the consensual ideas.

Political and economic factors are interdependent. Economic circumstances can impel state activities away from the general requirements of continued capitalist activity. Faced with particularly pressing demands from disadvantaged groups or facing extreme economic circumstances, a government may be more willing to countenance policies which would, in the long term, be disruptive of class dominance. It is for this reason that long-term political dominance must depend upon the pattern of political rule. Through participation in the decision-making bodies of the state – as members of the power elite who draw up policies, translate them into laws and regulations, and are involved in their enforcement – members of the capitalist class can help to ensure that the operations of the state are brought back into line as soon as possible and so do not undermine continued class dominance.

It is also through the ability of members of the capitalist class to exert influence on the state from outside that economic constraints, cultural consensus, and political rule are able to work in the same direction. Through the informal mechanisms of the establishment and through more formal methods of interest representation, capitalist interests are articulated within the state. Business interests

have increasingly been brought together into highly organized pressure groups capable of engaging in propaganda on behalf of business
and of lobbying the state to promote its preferred policies. Successful
propaganda campaigns were run against the proposed nationalization of the sugar industry in the early 1950s and the banks in the
1970s.

Propagandizing and lobbying comprise what Domhoff has termed
the special interest process.[40] This process concerns the pressuring
of the state in an attempt to secure short-term interests and goals
such as contracts, subsidies, tax concessions, and other administrative decisions which are favourable to the particular interests of a
specific enterprise or the sectional interests of a specific category of
enterprises. Businesses use direct lobbying of the state at all levels,
employing lobbyists, lawyers, and others to act on their behalf, and
they back this up through a network of formal and informal contacts,
such as consultations, meetings, and working lunches. The complex
of informal connections range from the licit to the illicit – favours,
gifts and bribes are not uncommon supports of the general 'give-
and-take' of business relationships.

This extensive range of contacts is made possible by the circulation
of personnel between business and the state: retired civil servants
join business enterprises; government bodies and enterprises are
involved in interlocking board memberships; and there is considerable career mobility between state and corporate bureaucracies at
all levels of the managerial hierarchy. In these ways is built up a
common framework of understanding within which active lobbying
can take place. Businesses deal with state officials who have a real
knowledge of business.

The major foci of lobbying are the regulatory agencies which
affect the day-to-day operations and profit opportunities of
enterprises, and the advisory bodies which shape the general conditions under which they act. The fact that the interests pursued
are specific and sectional, and are therefore competing, has led
many analysts to see the existence of lobbying as lending support
to a pluralist view of power – evidence, at best, for the existence
of a fragmentary or segmented power elite. It remains the case,
nevertheless, that this competition is constrained within a framework
of general business interests, and that non-business interests are far
less likely to be successful in their lobbying.

The power of business is further enhanced through membership
of advisory bodies. As 'experts', members of the inner circle of
finance capitalists are co-opted by governments on to the plethora

of advisory and consultative bodies which play a key role in policy formulation. Though the number of such bodies has been reduced during the life of the Thatcher government, they are still numerous. These bodies include permanent councils, authorities, and committees, as well as numerous temporary committees, enquiries, and commissions.

Financial support for parties and candidates is a further mechanism of organized business influence. Where lobbying and membership of advisory bodies are predominantly concerned with influencing the policies of an existing government and other branches of the state elite, financial support for candidates and parties is primarily aimed at influencing political party policies and improving the electoral prospects of preferred parties. They are also means of securing control over parties and candidates once elected. The 'fat cats and money raisers'[41] attempt to form cliques to structure donations which influence the selection of candidates and their ability to pursue an electoral campaign.

The finances of the Conservative party depend heavily on funds provided by business enterprises, the party receiving these funds directly from large enterprises and indirectly from fund-raising organizations such as the Economic League and British United Industrialists. These two organizations are the main recipients of corporate funds, channelling them through the Conservative party and propaganda agencies. Particularly important as donors are the banking and insurance industries and the manufacturers of food, drink, and tobacco, and research has found that the size of a donation is related to how well integrated a company is into the business network. Those enterprises with extensive business connections through interlocking directorships are especially likely to give money to the fund-raising organizations, suggesting an important role for finance capitalists in the mobilization of political donations. Direct donations from business to the Conservative party come especially from the merchant banks and those enterprises which have close board-level links with these banks, suggesting again the role of political mediation played by finance capitalists on bank boards. These very same people tend to hold positions on the boards and committees of the fund-raising and propaganda organizations, where they are able to control the ways in which their funds are used. Their role in this process seems to be well recognized by the government, as they are far more likely to be the recipients of titles and honours than are other directors: a study of honours and donations over the period 1979–82 found that all eight peerages and

20 of the 33 knighthoods awarded to directors in the period went to directors of enterprises which were donors to the Conservative party.

These processes of lobbying and financing were formerly handled on a personal basis through the informal networks of the establishment. Kinship and friendship, cemented through frequent informal interaction, were the basis on which influence was exercised and funds were solicited. The decline of the establishment has given formal mechanisms of influence a more important role. During the 1960s and 1970s this involved the emergence of 'corporatist' structures of interest representation: organizations, committees, and agencies which brought together government, business, and, to a limited extent, trades unions on a formal basis for discussions. Britain developed a system of 'bargained corporatism', a 'corporate bias' within which competing pressure groups came together in central forums of interest representation such as the CBI and the TUC.[42]

The growth of this corporatist bias in political representation was part and parcel of the consolidation of the post-war 'Keynesian' or social democratic consensus. Both the Conservative and the Labour parties were agreed around a set of welfare and economic goals which were geared towards the maintenance of full employment and the promotion of economic growth. The achievement of these goals became progressively more difficult during the 1970s, and alternative political perspectives became stronger. Within the Conservative party, a radical liberal perspective was strong enough to be a compelling force in shaping the policies of the Heath government of the early 1970s. Commitment to this view among Conservative members was, however, less than full, and the attempt to introduce more competitiveness in the economy and to dismantle state regulatory controls was followed by a sharp 'U-turn' when the policies failed to achieve any short-term economic success. The subsequent electoral failure of the Heath government in 1974 helped to shift the ideological centre of gravity in the party towards the radical liberals, who centred their claims around the tenets of monetarism. The radicals successfully countered Heath in the party leadership elections and Margaret Thatcher became the focal point for carrying through the re-orientation of Conservative thought.

The commitment of the Labour government of the late 1970s to an increasingly monetarist position laid the basis in government policy for the full radical programme of the Conservatives after the election of 1979. Central to this development was the ideological

Plate 6.3 The CBI Conference at Brighton. (Reproduced by kind permission of Camera Press London: photograph by Jon Blau.)

framework which has come to be described as 'Thatcherism', a policy of 'authoritarian populism' stressing minimal but strong government.[43] This was the basis of a reconstructed electoral bloc which sustained the Thatcher government for more than a decade. It also led to a shift in the composition and outlook of the power bloc, which gave greater emphasis to commercial and multinational capital rather than to the interests of domestic industry. This involved a loosening of the framework of corporatist bias, a move away from concertation and towards a greater reliance on pressure-group politics.[44]

Michael Useem has sought to apply the ideas of such writers as Domhoff to the British situation. He sees the 'inner circle' of finance capitalists as the key element in the transformation of social cohesion into policy cohesion through the corporatist bodies and pressure groups. The major policy-planning and consensus-seeking organizations that Useem identifies in Britain are the Association of British Chambers of Commerce, the Institute of Directors, the British Institute of Management, and the Confederation of British Industry. Members of the inner circle are three times more likely to participate at the top levels of these organizations than are other directors, and they are especially well-represented at the very top levels. These organizations, he argues, are central to the formulation of business policy and many other public policy issues. They have good access to government decision-making and are able to ensure that their voice is heard where it matters: 'these associations constitute the formal interface between the highest levels of government and large corporations in all sectors, those who guide their activities can have a decisive impact on the public policies collectively promoted or opposed by business'.[45]

Useem argues that the consensus and planning organizations on which members of the inner circle are so heavily represented comprise 'the leading edge of business political activity'. They are the foundation upon which diverse and sectional interests are welded together and a consensual business point of view is formulated. For this reason, they are crucial in determining the part played by those of their members who enter more directly and more formally into the political world and become the spokespersons for business as a whole. They mould a 'class-wide' point of view, rather than a parochial or sectional viewpoint. They have a firm understanding of aggregate corporate opinion, and they have a good understanding of the political environment in which business operates. As a result, they 'hold views that reflect the broader thinking of the business community', they represent 'class-wide' interests rather than the narrower sectional interests of particular enterprises and industries.[46]

The class perspective of the members of the inner circle of finance capitalists in Britain may be said to embody a 'City' point of view on economic and political affairs. They represent the fusion of banking and industry to create the system of finance capital which was described in Chapter 4, and their views, as refracted through the practices of the enterprises which they direct, are oriented to short-term commercial considerations. The financial institutions of the City of London which now dominate the ownership and control of large enterprises have come increasingly to be concerned with short-term dividend and capital gains rather than with long-term capital appreciation. They have constrained those enterprises in which they invest to yield these short-term benefits, and these firms seek to generate improvements in their share price through such means as takeover bids rather than to invest their surplus funds in the improvement of their technology. The much-cited under-funding of British industry, therefore, is rooted in the spread of this City point of view throughout the whole of the inner circle of finance capitalists.[47]

The debate over the role of the City of London in the British economy has often involved the misleading idea of a split between 'finance' and 'industry', between distinct fractions of capital.[48] This is far from the truth. In fact, the important structural separation is that between big business and small and medium business. The sphere of big business is, to a considerable degree, the sphere of finance capital and the finance capitalists. It is here that the City point of view prevails – in the boardrooms of food manufacturers, steel producers, and television companies, as well as those of banks and insurance companies. The City point of view, rooted in short-term commercialism, involves a commitment to free international capital flows, stable sterling exchange rates, and tight monetary controls.[49] Though not unchallenged by the more 'multinational' orientations found in the boardrooms of the foreign-owned companies, this City point of view has exerted a considerable influence over government policy. 'Thatcherism' and its policy of market liberalization has had its greatest impact in the City, where the old informal and customary ways of doing business have almost completely given way to more formal and contractual relations. The so-called 'Big Bang' restructuring of the City of London transformed City enterprises and, through the influx of foreign capital, substantially strengthened the linkage of the British economy to global financial and commercial processes. As the dominant segment of the capitalist class in Britain, the inner circle plays a key role in articulating capitalist interests within the power elite. They are the planners and co-ordinators of the economy. Through their political participation, their informal contacts with the state, and their role in lobbying and party finance, they translate the City point of view into a dominant influence over state policies.

The question 'Who Rules Britain?' can now be answered. Britain is ruled by a capitalist class whose economic dominance is sustained by the operations of the state and whose members are disproportionately represented in the power elite which rules the state apparatus. That is to say, Britain does have a ruling class. Much remains to be done in documenting the anatomy and personnel of this class, but the general picture is, I believe, clear. For much of the first half of the present century, industrial interests remained subordinate within the class: economically the commercial interests of the City of London predominated and culturally the landowners prevailed. The cultural dominance of the landowners was expressed in the existence of high society, and its political alignment with City interests comprised the political form described as the establishment. The capitalist business class achieved full fusion as banking and industry fused to form finance capital. From the 1930s, finance capital came increasingly to be organized around institutional share ownership and the system of impersonal property. This transformation of the economy led to a change in the structure of the capitalist class. Instead of being organized around an upper circle of status superiors, the capitalist class became organized around an inner circle of finance capitalists. This inner circle, espousing the City point of view, predominates in the formulation of state and business policy.

Notes

INTRODUCTION

1. A small selection of the many books published are: R. Perrott, *The Aristocrats* (Weidenfeld & Nicolson, London, 1968); A. Sinclair, *The Last of the Best* (Weidenfeld & Nicolson, London, 1968); and S. Winchester, *Their Noble Lordships* (Faber & Faber, London, 1981).
2. W. L. Guttsman, *The British Political Elite* (MacGibbon & Kee, London, 1963).
3. A. Sampson, *The Anatomy of Britain* (1962), *The Anatomy of Britain Today* (1965), *The New Anatomy of Britain* (1971), *The Changing Anatomy of Britain* (1982), (all Hodder & Stoughton, London).
4. R. Miliband, *The State in Capitalist Society*, (Weidenfeld & Nicolson, London, 1969).
5. C. W. Mills, *The Power Elite*, (Oxford University Press, New York, 1956), p. 277.
6. See the important recent contribution in B. Turner, *Status* (Open University Press, Milton Keynes, 1988).
7. The concept of power is one of the most complex in sociology. The most recent, and most promising work in this area is S. R. Clegg, *Frameworks of Power* (Sage, London, 1989).
8. G. W. Domhoff, *Who Rules America* (Prentice-Hall, Englewood Cliffs, 1967).
9. Chapter 3 extends the more detailed account given in J. Scott, *The Upper Classes* (Macmillan, London, 1982). In that book I sidestepped many of the theoretical ideas set out in this book. In particular, I deliberately avoided the use of the concepts 'ruling class' and 'elite', believing them to be irredeemably muddled. The present book recognizes that the terms have valid uses in social research, if only their meanings can be clarified. It should be noted that I no longer use the

term 'upper class', except where this is the self-description of a particular group. Instead I use the more meaningful concept of a capitalist class.

10. The most important general surveys from which to begin can be found in the work of T. B. Bottomore: *Classes in Modern Society* (Allen & Unwin, London, 1965); *Elites and Society* (C. A. Watts, London, 1964). An important recent source is *The Capitalist Class*, ed. T. B. Bottomore and R. Brym, (Harvester-Wheatsheaf, Brighton, 1989). I am grateful to Tom Bottomore for reading and commenting on the manuscript of this book.

Chapter 1   What is a Capitalist Class?

1. The quote is taken from T. B. Bottomore and M. Rubel, *Karl Marx: Selected Writings in Sociology and Social Philosophy* (Penguin, Harmondsworth, 1963 [1st edn, 1956]), p. 207.
2. Ibid., p. 186.
3. K. Renner, *The Institutions of Private Law and their Social Function* (Routledge & Kegan Paul, London, 1949 [1st edn, 1904]); R. Hilferding, *Finance Capital* (Routledge & Kegan Paul, London, 1981 [1st edn, 1910]).
4. D. Bell, *The End of Ideology* (Collier-Macmillan, New York, 1961); J. K. Galbraith, *The New Industrial State* (Hamish Hamilton, London, 1967).
5. S. Aaronovitch, *The Ruling Class* (Lawrence & Wishart, London, 1961), p. 33, emphasis removed.
6. Ibid., pp. 40–1, 87–8.
7. A review of the history and development of Fabianism can be found in M. Cole, *The Story of Fabian Socialism* (Heinemann, London, 1961). See also A. H. Halsey, 'Provincials and Professionals: The British Post-war Sociologists', in *Essays on the History of British Social Research*, ed. M. Bulmer (Cambridge University Press, 1985).
8. G. B. Shaw, Second Fabian Tract (Fabian Society, London, 1884).
9. The quotes are from R. H. Tawney, *Equality* (Allen & Unwin, London, 1964 [1st edn,, 1931]), p. 164, and G. B. Shaw, *The Intelligent Woman's Guide to Socialism, Capitalism, Sovietism and Fascism* (Penguin, Harmondsworth [1st edn, 1928]), 1937, p. 181.
10. T. Veblen, *The Theory of the Leisure Class* (Mentor, New York, 1953 [1st edn, 1899]).
11. Shaw, *Intelligent Woman's Guide*, p. 72.
12. J. Burnham, *The Managerial Revolution* (John Day, New York, 1941). This section draws on the Introduction to *The Sociology of Elites*, ed. J. Scott, vol. 2 (Edward Elgar Publishing, Cheltenham, 1990).
13. Tawney, *Equality*; D. V. Glass, *Social Mobility in Britain* (Routledge & Kegan Paul, London, 1951).

14. These arguments are contained in three essays, 'The Composition of the Middle Classes' (1950), 'The Social Structure of England' (1951), and 'Elites in the British Class Structure' (1955), all of which are printed in G. D. H. Cole, *Studies in Class Structure* (Routledge & Kegan Paul, London, 1955).

15. Cole, *Studies in Class Structure*, pp. 63–4.

16. Ibid., p. 69.

17. See C. A. R. Crosland, *The Future of Socialism* (Jonathan Cape, London, 1956), and idem., *The Conservative Enemy* (Cape, London, 1962).

18. The counterpart to Crosland's acceptance of managerialism was his acceptance of the 'embourgeoisement' thesis of the affluent worker. This is fully and critically discussed in J. H. Goldthorpe, D. Lockwood, F. Bechhofer, and J. Platt, *The Affluent Worker in the Class Structure* (Cambridge University Press, London, 1969).

CHAPTER 2   WHAT IS A RULING CLASS?

1. *Karl Marx: Selected Writings*, ed. Bottomore and Rubel, pp. 138, 93.

2. K. Marx and F. Engels, *On Britain* (Lawrence & Wishart, London, 1954), p. 404. The sections quoted from this book date from 1855 to 1863. See especially pp. 349–355, 404–408, 409–413.

3. Ibid., pp. 407, 409.

4. Ibid., p. 410.

5. Ibid., p. 411.

6. Ibid., pp. 491–2, 493.

7. Ibid., p. 499.

8. S. Haxey, *Tory MP* (Victor Gollancz, London, 1939).

9. Ibid., p. 40.

10. Ibid., p. 180.

11. S. Aaronovitch, *The Ruling Class*, p. 134.

12. Ibid., p. 149.

13. Ibid., pp. 157, 154–5.

14. Miliband, *State in Capitalist Society*, p. 51. (References are to the Coronet paperback edition).

15. Ibid., p. 54.

16. Ibid., p. 37. See also R. Miliband, *Capitalist Democracy in Britain* (Oxford University Press, London, 1982), p. 5.

17. Miliband, *State in Capitalist Society*, p. 45.

18. J. H. Westergaard and H. Resler, *Class in a Capitalist Society* (Heinemann, London, 1975), pp. 92, 95, 346ff.

19. Miliband, *State in Capitalist Society*, p. 61.

20. Miliband, *Capitalist Democracy*, p. 7.

21. A. Giddens, *Capitalism and Modern Social Theory* (Cambridge University Press, 1971), p. 36. Giddens drraws here on the arguments of

Wesołowski, which I discuss more fully in Chapter 6. A number of important issues raised in this section are discussed in T. B. Bottomore, 'The Capitalist Class', in *The Capitalist Class*, ed. Bottomore and Brym.

22. N. Poulantzas, 'The Problem of the Capitalist State', *New Left Review*, 58 (1969); idem., 'The Capitalist State: A Reply to Miliband and Laclau', *New Left Review*, 95 (1976); R. Miliband, 'The Capitalist State', *New Left Review*, 59 (1970); idem., 'Poulantzas and the Capitalist State', *New Left Review*, 82 (1973). This whole discussion draws heavily on ideas set out in A. Gramsci, *Selections from the Prison Notebooks*, ed. Q. Hoare and G. Nowell Smith, (Lawrence & Wishart, London, 1971).

23. N. Poulantzas, *Political Power and Social Classes* (New Left Books, London, 1973 [originally 1968]), and idem., *State, Power, Socialism* (Verso, London, 1978). See also R. Q. Gray, 'Bourgeois Hegemony in Victorian Britain', in *Class, Hegemony and Party*, ed. J. Bloomfield (Lawrence & Wishart, London, 1977). See the important discussion in J. Urry, *The Anatomy of Capitalist Society* (Macmillan, London, 1981), pp. 53–4, 83–4.

24. Westergaard and Resler, *Class in a Capitalist Society*, p. 258.

25. This is discussed further in the Introduction to *Sociology of Elites*, ed. Scott, vol. I. See also Bottomore, *Elites and Society* and G. Parry, *Political Elites* (Allen & Unwin, London, 1969) E. A. Albertoni, *Mosca and the Theory of Elitism* (Blackwell, Oxford, 1987).

26. A. Giddens, 'Elites in the British Class Structure', *Sociological Review*, 20, 3 (1972), pp. 345–372. The references which follow are to the reprint in *Elites and Power in British Society*, ed. P. Stanworth and A. Giddens (Cambridge University Press, London, 1974).

27. Ibid., p. 4.

28. Giddens, *Capitalism and Modern Social Theory*, p. 12.

29. Miliband, *State in Capitalist Society*, p. 51.

30. Ibid., Chapter 3. I have slightly modified Miliband's categories.

31. It is important to note that the institutional hierarchies of the political parties themselves are not included in the state elite. They are private bodies outside the state, and their power in relation to government and representative assemblies is a question for empirical investigation.

32. Miliband, confusingly, includes the heads of the nationalized enterprises under this heading. In view of their legal distinctiveness from the state – they are not civil servants – they should be regarded as outside the formally-defined state system.

33. A similar view of the power elite can be found in the important work of W. Wesołowski, *Classes, Strata, and Power* (Routledge & Kegan Paul, London, 1979 [originally 1966]), pp. 51–2. It should be noted that my usage departs somewhat from that of Mills, where the idea of

11. H. Perkin, *The Origins of Modern English Society, 1780–1880* (Routledge & Kegan Paul, London, 1969), p. 49.
12. Clark, *English Society*, p. 78. See also H. Newby, 'The Deferential Dialectic', *Comparative Studies in Society and History*, 17 (1975).
13. Laslett recognizes this central status division, but misleadingly describes it as the class boundary of a 'one class society'. See P. Laslett, *The World We have Lost*, 2nd edn (Methuen, London, 1961).
14. T. Nairn, *The Breakup of Britain* (London, New Left Books, 1977), and idem., *Enchanted Glass* (Hutchinson Radius, London, 1988). See also N. Abercrombie, S. Hill, and B. Turner, *The Dominant Ideology Thesis* (Allen & Unwin, London, 1980).
15. Mingay, *English Landed Society*, pp. 113–5. See also Clark, *English Society* and the rather different view of L. Namier, *The Structure of Politics at the Accession of George III* (Macmillan, London, 1957 [1st edn, 1928]).
16. E. P. Thompson, *The Making of the English Working Class*, (Penguin, Harmondsworth, 1963); J. Foster, *Class Struggle in the Industrial Revolution* (Weidenfeld & Nicolson, 1974).
17. Perkin, *Origins of Modern English Society*. The whole of my discussion draws extensively on Perkin's description of 'the birth of class'. See also Abercrombie et al., *Dominant Ideology Thesis*, pp. 97ff.
18. B. Moore, *Social Origins of Dictatorship*.
19. S. Beer, *Modern British Politics* (Faber & Faber, London, 1965), pp. 43–54.
20. W. D. Rubinstein, *Men of Property* (Croom Helm, London, 1981).
21. Guttsman, *British Political Elite*, pp. 38–41.
22. Abercrombie et al., *Dominant Ideology Thesis*, pp. 102 ff.

CHAPTER 4   IS THERE STILL A CAPITALIST CLASS?

1. This argument is elaborated in J. Scott, *Corporations, Classes and Capitalism* 2nd edn (Hutchinson, London, 1985), ch. 8. A related argument, though using different terminology, can be found in J. Urry, *The Anatomy of Capitalist Society* (Macmillan, London, 1981), pp. 66–71.
2. This distinction between 'control' and 'rule' in corporate enterprises is elaborated in J. Scott, 'Corporate Control and Corporate Rule: Britain in an International Perspective', *British Journal of Sociology*, 45 (1990).
3. See the argument in N. Abercrombie and J. Urry, *Capital, Labour and the Middle Classes* (Allen & Unwin, London, 1983). See also J. Goldthorpe, 'On the Service Class, Its Function and Future', in *Social Class and the Division of Labour*, ed. A. Giddens and G. Mackenzie (Cambridge University Press, 1983).
4. The case of commercial landlords is, of course, different, and this is why I have written of 'homes' rather than 'houses'. The commercial

the power elite was introduced as an *alternative* to the
the ruling class. See Mills, *The Power Elite*.
34. See Miliband's notion of the 'partnership' between the
    classes in 'State Power and Class Interests', *New Le*
    (1983), p. 65.
35. Note that this statement refers to higher levels of forma
    not, necessarily, to higher levels of effective power.

CHAPTER 3   THE MAKING OF THE RULING CLASS

1. A. Giddens, *The Nation State and Violence* (Polity Pres
   1985). This discussion draws also on the arguments of E.
   in *The Age of Revolution* (1962), *The Age of Capital* (1
   Age of Empire (1987) (all: Weidenfeld & Nicolson, Lo
2. See the discussion of these points in B. Moore, *Soc
   Dictatorship and Democracy* (Penguin, Harmondsworth,
   1966]). See also A. Macfarlane, *The Origins of English*
   (Basil Blackwell, Oxford, 1978).
3. A. J. Mayer, *The Persistence of the Old Regime* (Croor
   don, 1981), p. 81. Mayer makes the point that this v
   of France, where the nobility lost its formal monopol
   authority.
4. R. Nisbet, *The Sociological Tradition* (Basic Books, New
5. 'Elitism' is here used in its original and most genera
   normative legitimating framework for those who styled i
   'the best' in society. It should not be confused with the
   'state elite' and 'power elite' developed in the previous
6. See J. C. D. Clark, *English Society, 1688–1832* (Cambrid
   Press, 1985); M. Mann, 'A Controversy in Stratification
   Gender and Stratification, ed. R. Crompton and M. Mann
   Cambridge, 1986). And see M. Waters, 'Patriarchy and \
   Exploration and Reconstruction of Concepts of Masc
   nation', in *Sociology*, 23 (1989).
7. This section draws on Scott, *Upper Classes*, G. Mingay, *En
   Society in the Eighteenth Century* (Routledge & Kegan Pi
   1963), and L. Stone and J. F. Stone, *An Open Elite?* (Ox
   sity Press, 1984).
8. Mingay, *English Landed Society*, p. 26.
9. See Stone and Stone, *An Open Elite?*, pp. 46ff.
10. On the development and nature of the strict settlement
    English Landed Gentry, pp. 32–36; J. V. Beckett, *The A
    England, 1688–1832* (Basil Blackwell, Oxford, 1986) pp
    above all, L. C. Bonfield, *Marriage Settlements, 1601–1740*
    University Press, 1983).

uses of housing are similar to the other cases of commercial assets discussed below. For an alternative view of housing see P. Saunders, *A Nation of Home Owners* (Unwin Hyman, London, 1990).

5. The distinction between 'property for use' and 'property for power' comes from the work of A. H. Halsey. See the articles by Halsey and by Hird in *The Wealth Report*, ed. F. Field (Routledge & Kegan Paul, London, 1979) and idem., *The Wealth Report 2* (Routledge & Kegan Paul, London, 1983).

6. Large-scale entrepreneurial capitalists are here distinguished from the much greater number of members of the 'entrepreneurial middle class' which form an extended tail to an entrepreneurial interest which currently receives much support from the government. See R. Scase and R. Goffee, *The Entrepreneurial Middle Class* (Croom Helm, London, 1982).

7. See Scott, 'Corporate Control and Corporate Rule'.

8. In earlier publications I referred to the executive capitalist as an 'internal capitalist'. The term 'executive capitalist' is, I now believe, more descriptive.

9. This is elaborated more fully in J. Scott and C. Griff, *Directors of Industry* (Polity Press, Cambridge, 1984), and J. Scott, *Capitalist Property and Financial Power* (Wheatsheaf, Hassocks, 1986).

10. See the discussion in M. R. Zeitlin, *The Large Corporation and Contemporary Classes* (Polity Press, Cambridge, 1989).

11. Evidence on land ownership can be found in D. Massey and A. Catalano, *Capital and Land* (Edward Arnold, London, 1978), and H. Newby, *Green and Pleasant Land?* (Hutchinson, London, 1979).

12. Evidence on modern farming can be found in H. Newby, C. Bell, D. Rose and P. Saunders, *Property, Paternalism, and Power* (Hutchinson, London, 1978), and in Newby, *Green and Pleasant Land?*

13. See M. R. Zeitlin and R. Ratcliff, *Landlords and Capitalists* (Princeton University Press, 1988), ch. 1.

14. See the discussion of this in Scott and Griff, *Directors of Industry*, ch. 3.

15. The material for this case study is drawn predominantly from I. Harford et al., *The Making of a Ruling Class* (Benwell Community Project, Newcastle, 1978). The transformation of the Scottish economy and Scottish business is discussed in detail in J. Scott and M. Hughes, *The Anatomy of Scottish Capital* (Croom Helm, London, 1980).

16. His great grandson was, until currently, 1990, a member of the government.

17. See the discussion in Scott, *Corporations, Classes and Capitalism*, and idem., 'Corporate Control and Corporate Rule'.

18. M. Useem, *The Inner Circle* (Oxford University Press, New York, 1984).

19. On merchant banking see M. Lisle-Williams, 'Beyond the Market: The

Survival of Family Capitalism in the English Merchant Banks', and idem., 'Merchant Banking Dynasties in the English Class Structure', *British Journal of Sociology*, 35 (1984), and reprinted in *Sociology of Elites*, ed. Scott, vol. 1.

20. This category also includes a small number of mutual insurance companies and some companies controlled by British corporate interests.
21. See Rubinstein, *Men of Property*.
22. The discussion that follows draws especially upon W. D. Rubinstein, *Wealth and Inequality in Britain* (Faber & Faber, London, 1986), ch. 2; C. D. Harbury and D. M. W. Hitchens, *Income and Wealth Inequality in Britain* (Allen & Unwin, London, 1979); A. B. Atkinson and A. J. Harrison, *The Distribution of Personal Wealth in Britain* (Cambridge University Press, 1978). See also J. Rentoul, *The Rich Get Richer* (Unwin Hyman, London, 1987). See also the general discussion in D. Coates, 'Britain', in *The Capitalist Class* ed. Bottomore and Brym.
23. S. Schifferes, 'The Rich in Britain', supplement to *New Society*, 22 Aug. 1986; *Social Trends*, 19 (1989), Table 5.24.
24. Lord Portman, listed in the top 20, is the father of Lady Anne Cavendish-Bentinck.
25. Harbury and Hitchens, *Income and Wealth Inequality*, chs 3 and 4.
26. This is elaborated in Scott, *Corporations, Classes, and Capitalism*, and idem., *Capitalist Property and Financial Power*, pp. 88–93.
27. The evidence for this section is drawn from Newby, *Green and Pleasant Land?*, ch. 2; Massey and Catalano, *Capital and Land*; H. Clemenson, *English Country Houses and Landed Estates* (Croom Helm, London, 1982).
28. A similar argument about the dissociation of capital and class reproduction, though cast in different terminology, can be found in S. Clegg, P. Boreham, and G. Dow, *Class, Politics and the Economy* (Routledge & Kegan Paul, London, 1986), ch. 5.

Chapter 5   Is there still an Upper Circle?

1. My discussion of the development of 'Society' here and throughout this chapter draws heavily on the important work of L. Davidoff, *The Best Circles* (Croom Helm, London, 1973). See also L. Davidoff and C. Hall, *Family Fortunes* (Hutchinson, London, 1987).
2. The development of this and similar directories is discussed in J. Scott, *A Matter of Record* (Polity Press, Cambridge, 1990), ch. 7.
3. Davidoff, *Best Circles*, p. 25.
4. A. Sproule, *The Social Calendar* (Blandford Press, London, 1978).
5. Hunting was the only sport which involved any significant female participation.
6. Davidoff, *Best Circles*.
7. D. Cannadine, 'The British Monarchy and the "Invention of Tradition"

c., 1820–1977', in *The Invention of Tradition*, ed. E. J. Hobsbawm and T. Ranger (Weidenfeld & Nicolson, London, 1983); Nairn, *Enchanted Glass*.

8. K. Middlemas, *The Pursuit of Pleasure* (Gordon & Cremonesi, London, 1977); S. Margetson, *The Long Party* (Gordon & Cremonesi, London, 1974).
9. A. Barr and P. York, *The Official Sloane Ranger Handbook* (Ebury Press, London, 1982); idem., *The Official Sloane Ranger Diary* (Ebury Press, London, 1983).
10. *Englishness: Politics and Culture*, ed. R. Colls and P. Dodd, (Croom Helm, London, 1986).
11. T. Heald, *Networks* (Hodder & Stoughton, London, 1983), p. 187.
12. J. Gathorne-Hardy, *The Public School Phenomenon* (Hodder & Stoughton, 1977).
13. Sampson, *Anatomy of Britain*.
14. This calculation is based on one leading member in each of the 200 families. The figures would have been higher if all adult members of the families had been analysed.
15. Sampson, *Changing Anatomy of Britain*, p. 143; Heald, *Networks*, pp. 47, 252. Heald gives 47 per cent as the figure for Eton.
16. Sampson, *Changing Anatomy of Britain*, p. 474.
17. P. Bourdieu, 'Cultural Reproduction and Social Reproduction (1971), in *Knowledge, Education, and Cultural Change*, ed. R. Brown (Tavistock, London, 1973); P. Bourdieu and J-C. Passeron, *Reproduction in Economy, Society and Culture* (Sage, London, 1977 [1st edn, 1970]).
18. Miliband, *State in Capitalist Society*, p. 59.
19. Useem, *Inner Circle*, p. 106.

CHAPTER 6   IS THERE STILL A RULING CLASS?

1. This figure draws on the attempt by Giddens to analyse the mechanisms of elite recruitment and integration, though it departs somewhat radically from his concepts. See Giddens, 'Elites in the British Class Structure', pp. 345–372. As I noted in Chapter 2, my usage of the term 'power elite' differs from that of Mills in *The Power Elite*, op. cit.
2. See R. A. Dahl, 'A Critique of the Ruling Elite Model' (1985), and W. Kornhauser, '"Power Elite" or "Veto Groups"' (1961), in *Sociology of Elites*, ed. Scott, vol. 1.
3. F. Parkin, *Marxism and Class Theory* (Tavistock, London, 1979), pp. 45ff.
4. Bourdieu and Passeron, *Reproduction in Economy, Society and Culture*; J. Marceau, *A Family Business?* (Cambridge University Press, 1989).
5. See M. Mann, 'Ruling Class Strategies and Citizenship', in *States, War,*

and Capitalism ed. M. Mann (Basil Blackwell, Oxford, 1988); R. Q. Gray, 'Bourgeois Hegemony in Victorian Britain'.

6. 'Conspiracy' is used to mean 'coordination', it does not mean that the bloc forms a tight conspiring cabal.
7. C. W. Mills, *The Power Elite* (Oxford University Press, New York, 1959), p. 11.
8. Ibid., p. 19.
9. Domhoff, *Who Rules America?*; idem., *The Higher Circles* (Random House, New York, 1970).
10. G. W. Domhoff, 'Social Clubs, Policy-Planning Groups, and Corporations', *Insurgent Sociologist*, 5, 3 (1975), p. 175.
11. See Scott, *Upper Classes*, pp. 106–7, and see Chapter 5 above.
12. C. Dandeker, *Surveillance, Power, and Modernity* (Polity Press, Cambridge, 1990), ch. 3.
13. Guttsman, *British Political Elite*, p. 79.
14. R. W. Johnson, 'The British Political Elite, 1955–1972', *European Journal of Sociology*, 14, 1 (1973), reprinted in *Sociology of Elites*, ed. Scott.
15. The use of male language is deliberate.
16. P. Stanworth, 'Elites and Privilege', in *U.K. Society*, ed. P. Abrams and R. Brown (Weidenfeld & Nicolson, London, 1984), p. 257.
17. Sampson, *Anatomy of Britain*, p. 175. Although widely attributed to Macmillan, the words 'You have never had it so good' involved a slight misquotation. In his speech to a Conservative rally in Bradford in 1957 he claimed that 'most of our people have never had it so good'.
18. The data on schooling relate to the status of the schools at the time that the ministers attended them. Some schools have subsequently changed status. In the count of university attendance, Lord Mackay is counted twice, as he attended both Edinburgh and Cambridge.
19. C. Mellors, *The British MP* (Farnborough, Saxon House, 1978); Scott, *Upper Classes*, table 7.4, p. 163.
20. The evidence in the following paragraph comes from studies summarized in Scott, *Upper Classes*, pp. 164–172, and Stanworth, 'Elites and Privilege', pp. 252–255. See in particular D. Boyd, *Elites and their Education* (NFER, London, 1973).
21. See figures reported in A. H. Halsey, A. F. Heath, and J. M. Ridge, *Origins and Destinations* (Clarendon Press, Oxford, 1980), p. 60; and J. Vaizey, 'The Public Schools', in H. Thomas, *The Establishment* (Blond, London, 1959), p. 26.
22. R. Miliband, *Parliamentary Socialism* (Merlin Press, London, 1973), idem., *Capitalist Democracy*, pp. 32ff., D. Coates, *Labour in Power?* (Longman, London, 1980).
23. G. Therborn, *What does the Ruling Class do when it Rules?* (New Left Books, London, 1978), pp. 144, 161.
24. Therborn, ibid., p. 160.

25. Therborn, ibid., p. 155.
26. Therborn, ibid., rejects the concept of a power bloc which I use here. He accepts, however, the reality and importance of joint participation in political power.
27. R. A. Dahl, *Who Governs?* (Yale University Press, New Haven, 1963), idem., 'Critique of the Ruling Elite Model'.
28. P. Bachrach and M. Baratz, *Power and Poverty* (Oxford University Press, New York, 1970), and C. Offe, 'The Theory of the Capitalist State and the Problem of Policy Formation', in L. N. Lindberg, R. Alford, C. Crouch, and C. Offe, *Stress and Contradiction in Modern Capitalism* (D. C. Heath, New York, 1975), pp. 125–144.
29. Westergaard and Resler, *Class in a Capitalist Society*, p. 142. See also J. Westergaard, 'Class, Inequality, and "Corporatism"', in *Class and Class Structure*, ed. A. Hunt (Lawrence & Wishart, London, 1977), pp. 182–184.
30. *Capitalism, State Formation and Marxist Theory*, ed. P. Corrigan, (Quartet, London, 1980).
31. I have described the formation and impact of such routines in relation to the production of state documents in Scott, *Matter of Record*.
32. Wesolowski, *Classes, Strata, and Power*; A. Gramsci, *Selections From the Prison Notebooks*, ed. Q. Hoare and G. Nowell Smith (Lawrence & Wishart, London, 1971).
33. Poulantzas, *State, Power, Socialism*, pp. 155–6.
34. R. Miliband, *Marxism and Politics* (Oxford University Press, London, 1977), p. 69. See also Westergaard and Resler, *Class in a Capitalist Society*, pp. 143–4, 249ff.
35. Abercrombie et al., *Dominant Ideology Thesis*, pp. 132–4.
36. Parkin, *Class Inequality and Political Order* (McGibbon & Kee, London, 1971), p. 83. For an important analysis of working-class deferentialism as an electoral support for the Conservative party see R. McKenzie and A. Silver, *Angels in Marble* (Heinemann, London, 1968).
37. See, for example, Miliband, *State in Capitalist Society*, and Giddens, 'Elites in the British Class Structure'.
38. W. Grant, *Business and Politics* (Macmillan, London, 1987), pp. 239–240.
39. Therborn, *What does the Ruling Class do*, pp. 166–7.
40. G. W. Domhoff, *The Powers that be* (Vintage Books, New York, 1979).
41. Domhoff, *Powers that be*, p. 143.
42. K. Middlemas, *Politics in an Industrial Society* (London, André Deutsch, 1979); Scott, *Corporations, Classes and Capitalism*, pp. 218ff.
43. *The Politics of Thatcherism*, ed. S. Hall and M. Jacques (Lawrence & Wishart, London, 1983).
44. Scott, *Corporations, Classes and Capitalism*, pp. 219–225.

45. Useem, *Inner Circle*, p. 72.
46. Ibid., p. 76.
47. The main views on economic decline are brought together in *The Economic Decline of Modern Britain*, ed. D. Coates and J. Hillard (Wheatsheaf, London, 1986).
48. See the debates in F. Longstreth, 'The City, Industry and the State', in *State and Economy in Contemporary Capitalism*, ed. C. Crouch (Croom Helm, London, 1979); M. Moran, 'Power, Policy and the City of London', in R. King, *Capital and Politics* (Routledge & Kegan Paul, London, 1983); G. K. Ingham, *Capitalism Divided* (Macmillan, London, 1984).
49. J. Coakley and L. Harris, *The City of Capital* (Basil Blackwell, Oxford, 1983); J. Scott, 'Ownership and Employer Control', in *Employment in Britain*, ed. D. Gallie (Basil Blackwell, Oxford, 1988).

Index